Get
Organized

By
Ron Fry

CAREER PRESS
3 Tice Road
P.O. Box 687
Franklin Lakes, NJ 07417
1-800-CAREER-1
201-848-0310 (NJ and outside U.S.)
FAX: 201-848-1727

Copyright © 1996 by Ron Fry

GET ORGANIZED

ISBN 1-56414-233-7, $6.99

Cover design by The Visual Group

Printed in the U.S.A. by Book-mart Press

To order this title by mail, please include price as noted above, $2.50 handling per order, and $1.00 for each book ordered. Send to: Career Press, Inc., 3 Tice Road, P.O. Box 687, Franklin Lakes, NJ 07417.

Or call toll-free 1-800-CAREER-1 (NJ and Canada: 201-848-0310) to order using VISA or MasterCard, or for further information on books from Career Press.

Library of Congress Cataloging-in-Publication Data

Fry, Ronald W.
    Get organized / by Ron Fry.
      p.   cm. -- (Ron Fry's how to study program)
    Includes index.
    ISBN 1-56414-233-7 (pbk.)
    1. Study skills--Handbooks, manuals, etc. 2. Students--Time management--Handbooks, manuals, etc. 3. Note-taking--Handbooks, manuals, etc.   I. Title. II. Series: Fry, Ronald W. How to study program.
LB1049.F735 1996
371.3'028'1--dc20   96-16320
                                                            CIP

Contents

Foreword

Start at the beginning

This year marks another major milestone in the near-decade long evolution of my *How to Study Program*—the addition of two new titles (this book and *Use Your Computer*) as well as the reissuance of new editions of *How to Study* (its fourth), *Improve Your Writing*, *Improve Your Reading*, *Improve Your Memory* and *"Ace" Any Test* (all in third editions). *Take Notes* and *Manage Your Time*, both still available in second editions, were not updated this year.

Why are these books the best-selling series of study guides ever published? Why are they still so *needed*, not only by students but by their parents who want so badly for them to do well?

Because virtually all of the conditions I've been writing and speaking about across the country since 1988 have remained...or gotten *worse:*

1. Despite modest recent improvements in test scores—in 1995, the average on the verbal portion of the SAT rose five points, math scores improved three points—U.S. students still score abysmally low compared to many other countries, especially on science and math tests.

2. Most parents, when polled, say improving our public schools is our nation's number one priority. Those same parents do *not* think public schools are doing a very good job teaching their kids much of anything.

3. Business leaders continue to complain that far too many entry-level job candidates can barely read, write, add or multiply. Many can't fill out job applications! As a result, businesses are spending billions to teach employees the basic skills they should have learned in school.

As a result, the need for my nine books will, unfortunately, continue, since they offer *exactly* the help most students need and their parents demand.

So who are you?

A number of you are students, not just the high school students I always thought were my readers, but also college students (a rousing plug for their high school preparation) and *junior* high school students (which says something far more positive about their eventual success).

Many of you reading this are adults. Some of you are returning to school. And some of you are long out of school but have figured out that if you could learn *now* the study skills your teachers never taught you, you'd do better in your careers—especially if you knew how to meet pressing deadlines or remember the key points of a presentation.

All too many of you are parents with the same lament: "How do I get Johnny to do better in school? If his life is as organized as his room, I fear for all of us!"

I want to briefly take the time to address every one of the audiences for this book and discuss some of the factors particular to each of you:

If you're a high school student

You should be particularly comfortable with both the language and format of this book—its relatively short sentences and paragraphs, occasionally humorous (hopefully) headings and subheadings, a reasonable but certainly not outrageous vocabulary. I wrote it with you in mind!

If you're a junior high school student

Learning *now* how to organize your studying and your life is key to success now and in the future. You are trying to learn how to study at *precisely* the right time. Sixth, seventh and eighth grades—before that sometimes cosmic leap to high school—are without a doubt the period in which these study skills should be mastered. If you're serious enough about studying to be reading this book, I doubt you'll have trouble with the concepts or the language.

If you're a "traditional" college student...

...having pretty much gone right from high school to college, learning how to organize your life and studies is not just a nice idea, it's the only thing that will enable you to survive. Trust me. You haven't even contemplated how busy life can be until you show up at old Klutzburg U. and get your first class schedule...and volunteer schedule...and athletics schedule...and work schedule.

If you're the parent of a student of any age

Your child's school is probably doing little if anything to teach him or her how to study. Which means he or she is not learning how to *learn*. And that means he or she is not learning how to *succeed*.

Should the schools be accomplishing that? Absolutely. After all, we spend $275 billion on elementary and secondary education in this country, *an average of $6,000 per student per year*. We ought to be getting more for that money than possible graduation, some football cheers and a rotten entry-level job market.

What can parents do?

There are probably even more dedicated parents out there than dedicated students, since the first phone call at any of my radio or TV appearances comes from a sincere and worried parent asking, "What can I do to help my kid do better in school?" Okay, here they are, the rules for parents of students of any age:

1. **Set up a homework area.** Free of distraction, well lit, all necessary supplies handy.

2. **Set up a homework routine.** When and where it gets done. Same bat-time every day.

3. **Set homework priorities.** Actually, just make the point that homework *is* the priority—before a date, before TV, before going out to play, whatever.

4. **Make reading a habit**—for them, certainly, but also for yourselves. Kids will inevitably do what you *do*, not what you *say* (even if you say *not* to do what you *do*).

5. **Turn off the TV.** Or at the very least, severely limit when and how much TV-watching is appropriate. This may be the toughest one.

6. **Talk to the teachers.** Find out what your kids are supposed to be learning. If you don't, you can't really supervise. You might even be teaching them things at odds with what the teacher's trying to do.

7. **Encourage and motivate**, but don't nag them to do their homework. It doesn't work.

8. **Supervise their work**, but don't fall into the trap of *doing* their homework.

9. **Praise them to succeed**, but don't overpraise them for mediocre work. Kids know when you're slinging it.

10. **Convince them of reality.** (This is for older students.) Okay, I'll admit it's almost as much of a stretch as turning off the TV, but learning and believing that the real world will not care about their grades, but measure them by what they know and what they can do, is a lesson that will save many tears (probably yours). It's probably never too early to (carefully) let your boy or girl genius get the message that life is not fair.

11. **If you can afford it, get your kid(s) a computer** and all the software they can handle. There really is no avoiding it: Your kids, whatever their age, absolutely must master technology (computers) in order to survive in and after school. A recent decade-long study has shown that kids who master computers learn faster and earn higher test scores.

The importance of your involvement

Your involvement in your child's education is absolutely essential to his or her eventual success. Surprisingly enough, the results of every study done in the last two decades about what affects a child's success in school clearly demonstrate that only one factor *overwhelmingly* affects it, every time: parental involvement. Not the size of the school, the money spent per pupil, the number of language labs, how many of the students go on to college, how many great teachers there are (or lousy ones). All factors, yes. *But none as significant as the effect you can have.*

So please, take the time to read this book (and all of the others in the series, but especially *How to Study*) yourself. Learn what your kids *should* be learning (and which of the other subject-specific books in the series your child needs the most).

And you can help tremendously, *even if you were not a great student yourself, even if you never learned great study skills*. You can learn now with your child—not only will it help him or her in school, it will help *you* on the job, whatever your field.

If you're a nontraditional student

If you're going back to high school, college or graduate school at age 25, 45, 65 or 85—you probably need the help these nine books offer more than anyone! Why? Because the longer you've been out of school, the more likely you don't remember what you've forgotten. And you've probably forgotten what you're supposed to remember! As much as I emphasize that it's rarely too early to learn good study habits, I must also emphasize that it's never too *late*.

If you're returning to school and attempting to carry even a partial courseload while simultaneously holding down a job, raising a family, or both, there are some particular problems you face that you probably didn't the first time you were in school:

Time and money pressures. Let's face it, when all you had to worry about was going to school, it simply *had* to be easier than going to school, raising a family and working for a living simultaneously. (And it was!) Mastering all of the techniques of time management is even more essential if you are to effectively juggle your many responsibilities to your career, family, clubs, friends, etc., with your commitment to school. Money management may well be another essential skill, whether figuring out how to pay for child care (something you probably didn't have to worry about the last time you were in school) or how to manage all your responsibilities while cutting your hours at work to make time for school.

Self-imposed fears of inadequacy. You may well convince yourself that you're just "out of practice" with all this school stuff. You don't even remember what to do with a highlighter! While some of this fear is valid, most is not. I suspect what many of you are really fearing is that you just aren't in that school "mentality" anymore, that you don't "think" the same way.

I think these last fears are groundless. You've been out there thinking and doing for quite a few years, perhaps very successfully, so it's really ridiculous to think school will be so different. It won't be. Relax.

Maybe you're worried because you didn't exactly light up the academic power plant the first time around. Well, neither did Edison or Einstein or a host of other relatively successful people. But then, you've changed rather significantly since those halcyon days of "boola boolaing," haven't you? Held a series of jobs, raised a family, saved money, taken on more and more responsibility? Concentrate on

11

how much *more* qualified you are for school *now* than you were *then!*

Feeling you're "out of your element." This is a slightly different fear, the fear that you just don't fit in any more. After all, you're not 18 again. But then, neither are fully half the college students on campus today. That's right, fully 50 percent of all college students are older than 25. The reality is, you'll probably feel more in your element now than you did the first time around!

You'll see teachers differently. Probably a plus. It's doubtful you'll have the same awe you did the first time around. At worst, you'll consider teachers your equals. At best, you'll consider them younger and not necessarily as successful or experienced as you are. In either event, you probably won't be quite as ready to treat your college professors as if they were akin to God.

There *are* differences in academic life. It's slower than the "real" world, and you may well be moving significantly faster than its normal pace. When you were 18, an afternoon without classes meant a game of Frisbee. Now it might mean catching up on a week's worth of errands, cooking (and freezing) a week's worth of dinners and/or writing four reports due last week. Despite your own hectic schedule, do not expect campus life to accelerate in response. You will have to get used to people and systems with far less interest in speed.

Some random thoughts about learning

Learning shouldn't be painful and certainly doesn't have to be boring, though it's far too often both. However, it's not necessarily going to be wonderful and painless, either. Sometimes you actually have to work hard to figure something out or get a project done. That *is* reality.

It's also reality that everything isn't readily apparent or easily understandable. That confusion reigns. Tell yourself that's okay and learn how to get past it. Heck, if you actually think you understand everything you've read the first time through, you're kidding yourself. Learning something slowly doesn't mean there's something wrong with you. It may be a subject that virtually everybody learns slowly.

A good student doesn't panic when something doesn't seem to be getting through the haze. He just takes his time, follows whatever steps apply and remains confident that the light bulb will indeed inevitably go off.

Parents often ask me, "How can I motivate my teenager?" My initial response is usually to smile and say, "If I knew the answer to that question, I would have retired very wealthy quite some time ago." However, I think there *is* an answer, but it's not something *parents* can do, it's something you, the student, have to decide: Are you going to spend the school day interested and alert or bored and resentful?

It's really that simple. Why not develop the attitude that you have to go to school anyway, so rather than being bored or miserable while you're there, you might as well be active and learn as much as possible? The difference between a C and an A or B for many students is, I firmly believe, merely a matter of wanting to do better. As I constantly stress in interviews, inevitably you will leave school. And very quickly, you'll discover the premium is on what you know and what you can do. Grades won't count anymore, neither will tests. So you can learn it all now or regret it later.

How many times have you said to yourself, "I don't know why I'm even trying to learn this (calculus, algebra, geometry, physics, chemistry, history, whatever). I'll *never* use this again!'"? I hate to burst bubbles, but unless you've got a patent on some great new fortune-telling device, you have *no clue* what you're going to need to know tomorrow or next week, let alone next year or next decade.

I've been amazed in my own life how things I did with no specific purpose in mind (except probably to earn money) turned out years later to be not just invaluable to my life or career but essential. How was I to know when I took German as my language elective in high school that the most important international trade show in book publishing, my field, was in Frankfurt...Germany? Or that the basic skills I learned one year working for an accountant (while I was writing my first book) would become essential when I later started four companies? Or how important basic math skills would be in selling and negotiating over the years? (Okay, I'll admit it: I haven't used a differential equation in 20 years, but, hey, you never know!)

So learn it *all*. And don't be surprised if the subject you'd vote "least likely to ever be useful" winds up being the key to *your* fame and fortune.

There are other study guides

Though I immodestly maintain my *How to Study Program* to be the most helpful to the most people, there are certainly lots of other purported study books out there. Unfortunately, I don't think many of them deliver what they promise. In fact, I'm actually getting mad at the growing number of study guides out there claiming to be "the sure way to straight As" or something of the sort. These are also the books that dismiss reasonable alternative ways to study and learn with, "Well, that never worked for me," as if that is a valid reason to dismiss it, as if we should *care* that it didn't work for the author.

Inevitably, these other books promote the authors' "system," which usually means what *they* did to get through school. This "system," whether basic and traditional or wildly quirky, may or may not work for you. So what do you do if "their" way of taking notes makes no sense to you? Or you master their highfalutin "Super Student Study Symbols" and still get Cs?

I'm not getting into a Dennis Miller rant here, but there are very few "rights" and "wrongs" out there in the study world. There's certainly no single "right" way to attack a multiple choice test or absolute "right" way to take notes. So don't get fooled into thinking there *is*, especially if what you're doing seems to be working for you.

Don't change what "ain't broke" just because some self-proclaimed study guru claims what you're doing is all wet. Maybe he's all wet. After all, if his system works for you, all it *really* means is you have the same likes, dislikes, talents or skills as the author.

Needless to say, don't read *my* books looking for the Truth—that single, inestimable system of "rules" that works for everyone. You won't find it, 'cause there's no such bird.

You *will* find a plethora of techniques, tips, tricks, gimmicks and what-have-you, some or all of which may work for you, some of which won't. Pick and choose, change and adapt, figure out what works for you. Because *you* are the one responsible for creating *your* study system, *not me*.

Yes, I'll occasionally point out "my way" of doing something. I may even suggest that I think it offers some clear advantages to all the alternative ways of accomplishing the same thing. But that *doesn't* mean it's some carved-in-stone, deviate-from-the-sacred-Ron-Fry-study-path-under-penalty-of-a-writhing-death kind of rule.

I've used the phrase "Study smarter, not harder" as a sort of catch-phrase in promotion and publicity for the **How to Study Program** for nearly a decade. So what does it mean to you? Does it mean I guarantee you'll spend less time studying? Or that the least amount of time is best? Or that studying isn't ever supposed to be hard?

Hardly. It does mean that studying inefficiently is wasting time that could be spent doing other (okay, probably more *fun)* things and that getting your studying done as quickly and efficiently as possible is a realistic, worthy and *attainable* goal. I'm no stranger to hard work, but I'm not a monastic dropout who thrives on self-flagellation. I try not to work harder than I have to!

In case you were wondering

Before we get on with all the tips and techniques necessary, let me make two important points about all nine study books.

First, I believe in gender equality, in writing as well as in life. Unfortunately, I find constructions such as "he and she," "s/he," "womyn" and other such stretches to be sometimes painfully awkward. I have therefore attempted to sprinkle pronouns of both genders throughout the text.

Second, you will find many pieces of advice, examples, lists and other words, phrases and sections spread throughout two or more of the nine books. In terms of this book, **Get Organized**, although brand-new, is very much a summary of the time-management, note-taking and basic organizational skills discussed previously throughout all of the other titles. As such, it duplicates, to a great extent, what was previously contained in the books **Take Notes** and **Manage Your Time**, neither of which have been updated this time around. If you've bought *this* book, you do *not* need to buy those *two*.

That said, I can guarantee that the nearly 1,200 pages of my *How to Study Program* contain the most wide-ranging, comprehensive and complete system of studying ever published. I have attempted to create a system that is usable, that is useful, that is practical, that is learnable. One that *you* can use—whatever your age, whatever your level of achievement, whatever your IQ—to start doing better in school, in work and in life *immediately*.

Ron Fry
May 1996

Chapter 1

The need for organization

Whether you're a high school student just starting to feel frazzled, a college student juggling five classes and a part-time job or a parent working, attending classes and raising a family, a simple, easy-to follow system of organization is crucial to your success. And despite your natural tendency to proclaim that you just don't have the *time* to spend scheduling, listing and recording, it's also the best way to give yourself *more* time.

Taking time to make time

I'm sure many of you reading this are struggling with your increasing responsibilities and commitments. Some of you may be so overwhelmed you've just given up. Those of you who haven't probably figure it's your fault—if you just worked *harder*, spent more time on your papers and assignments, set up camp in the library—then everything would work out.

So you resign yourselves to all-nighters, cramming for tests and forgetting about time-consuming activities like eating and sleeping. Trying to do everything—even when there's too much to do—without acquiring the skills to *control* your time, is an approach that will surely lead to burnout.

When does it all end?

With classes, homework, a part-time or full-time job, and all the opportunities for fun and recreation, life as a student can be very busy. But, believe me, it doesn't suddenly get easier when you graduate.

Most adults will tell you that it only gets *busier*. There will always be a boss who expects you to work later, children who need to be fed, clothed and taken to the doctor, hobbies and interests to pursue, community service to become involved in, courses to take, etc.

If you're an adult doing all of the latter, I sure don't have to tell you how important organization is, do I?

There may not be enough time for everything

When I asked one busy student if she wished she had more time, she joked, "I'm *glad* there are only 24 hours in a day. Any more and I wouldn't have an excuse for not getting everything done!"

Let me give you the good news: There *is* a way that you can accomplish more in less time. And it doesn't even take more effort. You can plan ahead and make conscious choices about how your time will be spent, and how much time you will spend on each task. You can have more control over your time, rather than always running out of time as you keep trying to do everything.

Now the bad news: The first step to managing your time should be deciding just what is important...and what isn't. Difficult as it may be, sometimes it's necessary for us to recognize that we truly *can't* do it all; to slice from our busy schedules those activities that aren't as meaningful to us so that we can devote more energy to those that are.

You may be a *Star Trek* fan from way back. But is it really the best use of your time to run back to your room to catch the morning rerun each weekday?

You may love music so much, you want to be in the school orchestra, jazz band, choir and play with your own garage band on weekends. But is it realistic to commit to all four?

Your job at the mall boutique may mean you get 20 percent off all the clothes you buy. But if you are working there four days a week, taking 15 hours of classes and working at the food co-op on weekends, when do you expect to study?

If you're raising a family, working part-time and trying to take a near-full class load yourself, it's probably time to cure yourself of the Super Mom syndrome.

But there is enough time to plan

Yet, even after paring down our commitments, most of us are still challenged to get it all done. What with classes, study time, work obligations, extracurricular activities and social life, it's not easy getting it all in—even without *Star Trek*.

The organizational plan that I outline in this book is designed particularly for students. Whether you're in high school, college or graduate school, a "traditional" student or one who's chosen to return to school after being out in the "real world" for a while, you'll find that this is a manageable program that will work for you.

This program allows for flexibility. In fact, I encourage you to adapt any of my recommendations to your own unique needs. That means it will work for you whether you are living in a dorm, sharing accommodations with a roommate or living with a spouse and children. That you *can* learn how to balance school, work, fun and even family obligations.

The purpose of this book is to help you make *choices* about what is important to you, set *goals* for yourself, *organize* and *schedule* your time and develop the *motivation* and *self-discipline* to follow your schedule and reach those goals, which will give you the time to learn all the other study skills I write about!

Wouldn't it be nice to actually have some *extra* time...instead of always running out of it?

To feel that you're exerting some control over your schedule, your schoolwork, your *life*...instead of caroming from appointment to appointment, class to class, assignment to assignment, like some crazed billiard ball?

It can happen.

I will not spend a lot of time trying to convince you that this is a "fun" idea—getting excited about calendars and to-do lists is a bit of a stretch. You will *not* wake up one morning and suddenly decide that organizing your life is just the most fun thing you can think of.

But I suspect you *will* do it if I can convince you that effective organization will reward you in some very tangible ways.

Presuming all this is true (and I'll wager it is), unless you have some darn good reasons—a solid idea of some of the benefits effective organization *can* bring you—you will probably find it hard to consistently motivate yourself to do it. It has to become a habit, something you do without thinking, but also something you do *no matter what.*

More work, less time, more fun!

An organizational or time management system that fits your needs can help you get more work done in less time. Whether your priority is more free time than you have now or improved grades, learning how to organize your life and your studies can help you reach your objective, because:

1. **It helps you put first things first.** Have you ever spent an evening doing a busy-work assignment for an *easy* class, only to find that you hadn't spend enough time studying for a crucial test in a more difficult one?

   Listing all of the tasks you are required to complete and *prioritizing* them ensures that the most important things will *always* get done—*even on days when you don't get* everything *done.*

2. **It helps you avoid time traps.** Time traps are the unplanned events that pop up, sometimes (it seems) every day. They're the fires you have to put out before you can turn to tasks like studying.

   You may fall into such time traps because they *seem* urgent...or because they seem *fun.* Or you may end up spending hours in them...without even realizing you're stuck.

   There is no way to avoid *every* time trap. But effective time management can help you avoid most of them. Time management is like a fire-*prevention* approach rather than a fire-*fighting* one: It allows you to go about your work systematically instead of moving from crisis to crisis or from whim to whim.

3. **It helps you anticipate opportunities.** In addition to helping you balance study time with other time demands, effective time management can help make the time you *do* spend studying more productive. You'll be able to get more done in the same amount of time or (even better) do more work in less time. I'm sure you could find *some* way to spend those extra hours each week.

   Imagine that you and another student are working on the same term paper assignment. You plan out the steps to be completed well in advance and start on them early. The other student delays even thinking about the paper until a week before the assignment is due.

   If both of you were unable to find all the materials you needed in the local library, you, who started early, would have the opportunity to send away for them. The student who had only a week left would not have the same luxury, or the same good grade.

4. **It gives you freedom and control.** Contrary to many students' fears, time management is *liberating,* not restrictive. A certain control over *part* of your day allows you to be flexible with the *rest* of your day.

   In addition, you will be able to plan more freedom into your schedule. For example, you would know well in advance that you have a big test the day after a friend's party. Instead of having to call your friend the night of the party with a big sob story, you could make sure you allocated enough study time beforehand and go to the party without feeling guilty, without even *thinking* about the test.

5. **It helps you avoid time conflicts.** Have you ever lived the following horror story? You get out of class at 5:30, remember you have a big math assignment due, *then* realize you have no time to do it since you have a music rehearsal at 6 p.m. *Then* you remember that your softball game is scheduled for 7 p.m...just before that date you made months ago (which you completely forgot about until you came home and found a not-so-subtle message on your answering machine).

    Simply having all of your activities, responsibilities and tasks written down in one place helps ensure that two or three things don't get scheduled at once. If time conflicts do arise, you will notice them well in advance and be able to rearrange things accordingly.

6. **It helps you avoid feeling guilty.** When you know how much studying has to be done and have the time scheduled to do it, you can relax—you *know* that the work will get done. It is much easier to forget about studying if you've already allotted the time for it. Without a plan to finish the work you are doing, you may feel like it's "hanging over your head"—even when you're not working on it. If you're going to spend time *thinking* about studying, you might as well just spend the time *studying!*

    Effective time management also helps keep your conscience off your back: When your studying is done, you can *really* enjoy your free time *without* feeling guilty because you're not studying.

7. **It helps you evaluate your progress.** If you know where you should be in class readings and assignments, you will never be surprised when deadlines loom. For example, if you've planned out the whole term and know you have to read an average of 75 pages a week to keep up in your business management class, and you only read 60 pages this week, you don't need a calculator to figure out that you are slightly behind. And it's easy enough to schedule a little more time to read next week so you can catch up to your schedule.

   On the other hand, if you only read when it doesn't cut into your leisure time (i.e., when your assignment doesn't conflict with your favorite TV programs) or until you're tired, you'll never know whether you're behind or ahead (but I'll bet you're behind!). Then one day you suddenly realize you have to be up to Chapter 7...by lunchtime.

8. **It helps you see the big picture.** Effective time management provides you with a bird's-eye view of the semester. Instead of being caught off guard when the busy times come, you will be able to plan ahead—*weeks* ahead—when you have big tests or assignments due in more than one class.

   Why not complete that German culture paper a few days early so it's not in the way when two other papers are due...or you're trying to get ready for a weekend ski trip? Conflicts can be worked out with fewer problems if you know about them in advance and do something to eliminate them.

9. **It helps you see the bigger picture.** Planning
   ahead and plotting your course early allows you
   to see how classes fit with your overall school
   career. For example, if you know you have to
   take chemistry, biology and pharmacology to be
   eligible for entrance into the nursing program,
   and the courses you will take later will build on
   those, you will at least be able to see why the
   classes are required for your major, even if you
   aren't particularly fond of one or two of them.

10. **It helps you learn how to study smarter,
    not harder.** Students sometimes think time
    management just means reallocating their
    time—spending the same time studying, the
    same time in class, the same time partying, just
    shifting around these time segments so
    everything is more "organized."

    This is only *partially* true—a key part of
    effective time management *is* learning how to
    prioritize tasks. But this simple view ignores
    one great benefit of taking control of your time:
    It may well be possible you will be *so* organized,
    so prioritized, *so in control of your time* that you
    can spend *less* time studying, get *better* grades
    and have *more* time for other things—
    extracurricular activities, hobbies, a movie,
    whatever.

    It's *not* magic, though it can *appear* magical.

It keeps getting better

Besides helping you to manage your time right now
and reach your immediate study goals, learning how to
organize your studying will *continue* to pay off.

Have you ever sat in a class and thought to yourself, "I'll *never* use this stuff once I get out of school"?

You won't say that about organizational skills. They will be useful throughout your life. Preparation is what school is all about—if you spend your time effectively now, you will be better prepared for the future.

And the better prepared you are, the more options you will have—effective learning and good grades *now* will increase your range of choices when you graduate. The company you work for or the graduate school you attend will be one *you* choose, not one whose choice was dictated by your poor past performance.

Learning how to manage your time now will develop habits and skills you can use outside of school. It may be difficult for you to develop the habits of effective time management, but don't think you're alone—time management presents just as much of a problem to many parents, professors and non-students. How many people do you know who *never* worry about time?

If you learn effective time management skills in school, the payoffs will come throughout your life. Whether you wind up running a household or a business, you will have learned skills you will use every day.

Time management is not a magic wand that can be waved to solve problems in school or after graduation. It is a craft that must be developed over time. There is no "time management gene" that you either have or lack, like the ones that produce brown eyes or black hair.

These techniques are tools that can be used to help you reach your short-term and long-range goals successfully.

The important thing to remember is that you *can* be a successful time manager and a successful student *if* you are willing to make the effort to learn and apply the principles in this book.

If you hate the idea of being tied to a schedule, if you fear that it would drain all spontaneity and fun from your life, I know you'll be pleasantly surprised when you discover that just the *opposite* is true.

Most students are relieved and excited when they learn what a liberating tool time management can be.

Let's explode some myths that may be holding *you* back.

Do I have to live in the library?

Learning effective organizational skills will not turn you into a study-bound bookworm. How much time do you need to set aside for studying? Ask your career counselor, and he or she will probably echo the timeworn 2:1 ratio—spend two hours studying *out* of class for every hour you spend *in* class.

Hogwash. That ratio may be way out of line—either not enough time or too much. The amount of study time will vary from individual to individual, depending on your classes, abilities, needs and goals.

Scheduling time to study doesn't mean that you have to go from three hours of studying a day to eight. In fact, laying out your study time in advance often means you can relax more when you're *not* studying because you won't be worrying about when you're going to get your schoolwork done—the time's been set aside.

How *long* you study is less important than how *effective* you are when you do sit down to study. The goal is not to spend *more* time studying, but to spend the same or less time, *getting more done in whatever time you spend.*

It's too complicated

Many fear that time management implies complexity. Actually, I recommend simplicity. The more complex your system, the harder it will be to use and, consequently, the less likely you *will* use it consistently. The more complex the system, the more likely it will collapse.

It's too inflexible

You can design your time management system to fit your own needs. Some of the skills you will learn in this book will be more helpful to you in reaching your goals than others. You may already be using some of them. Others you will want to start using right now. Still others may not fit your needs at all.

Use the skills that are most likely to lead you to *your* study goals, meet *your* needs and fit with *your* personality.

Inflexibility is most people's biggest fear—"If I set it all out on a schedule, then I won't be able to be spontaneous and choose what to do with my time later."

Your time management system can be as flexible as you want. In fact, the best systems act as guides, not some rigid set of "must do's" and "can't do's."

That's enough about the myths. Let's take a look at what is actually required to use your time management skills effectively.

A good notebook and a sharp pencil

You have to be able to look at your plan when it's time to use it. It's nearly impossible to make detailed plans very far in advance without having a permanent record. Make it your rule: "If I plan it out, I will write it down."

And make sure that you have *one place to write and keep all your schedule information,* including class times, meetings, study times, project due dates, vacations, doctor appointments, social events, etc., so you always know exactly where to find them.

Your readiness to adapt and personalize

The time management system that best suits you will be tailor-made to fit *your* needs and personality.

Consider the following example: While most parents turn the lights out and keep things quiet when their baby is trying to go to sleep, one baby I know, who spent two months in the hustle and bustle of a newborn intensive-care unit, couldn't sleep unless the lights were *on* and it was *noisy.*

Similarly, while many students will study best in a quiet environment, others may feel uncomfortable in a "stuffy" library and prefer studying in their living room.

Make your study schedule work for *you,* not your night-owl roommate who must plan every activity down to the minute. Alter it, modify it, make it stricter, make it more flexible. Whatever works for you.

You'll never be disorganized again!

We've all had the experience of missing an important appointment or commitment and saying, "I know I had that written down somewhere—I wonder *where?*"

It's easy to *think,* "I'll write it down so I won't forget," but a schedule that is not used regularly isn't a safety net at all. You must consistently write down your commitments. You must spend time filling out your schedule every week, every day.

Any efforts you make to manage your time will be futile if you do not have your schedule with you when you need it. For example, you are in art class without your schedule when your teacher tells you when your next project is due. You jot it down in your art notebook and promise yourself you'll add it to your schedule as soon as you get home.

You hurry to your next class, and your geology instructor schedules a study session for the following week. You scribble a reminder in your lab book.

Between classes, a friend stops to invite you to a party Thursday night. You promise you'll be there.

You arrive at work to find out your supervisor has scheduled your hours for the following week. She checks them with you, they seem fine, so you commit to them.

Had you been carrying your schedule with you, you would have been able to write down your art project and schedule the necessary amount of preparation time.

You would have realized that your geology study session was the same night as your friend's party and discovered that accepting the work schedule your supervisor presented left you with little time to work on your art project.

Take your schedule with you anywhere and everywhere you think you might need it.

When it doubt, take it along!

Keeping your schedule with you will reduce the number of times you have to say, "I'll just try to remember it for now" or "I'll write it down on this little piece of paper and transfer it to my planner later."

Always make a point of writing down tasks, assignments, phone numbers and other bits of important information in your schedule *immediately*.

Use your new system consistently

In order to test its effectiveness, you must give any time management system a chance to work—give it a trial run. No program can work unless it is utilized consistently. And consistency won't happen without effort.

It's just like learning to ride a bicycle. It's a pain at first; you may even fall down a few times. But once you're a two-wheel pro, you can travel much faster and farther than you could by foot.

The same goes for the techniques you will learn here—they may take practice and a little getting used to, but once you've lived a "reorganized" life for a couple of weeks, you'll probably find yourself in the habit of doing it. From then on, it will take relatively little effort to maintain.

That's when you'll really notice the payoff—when the task becomes second nature.

Chapter 2

Organize your life

In one of my all-time favorite Abbott & Costello routines, the hapless Costello stands in front of a huge rolltop desk. There are hundreds—no, *thousands*—of papers spilling out of it. Suddenly, Abbott, the supreme delegator, comes in and asks for "the Smerling contract, 1942." Costello pulls out a pair of enormous tongs, roots around in the cavernous desk, papers spilling everywhere, and pulls out a single sheet of paper. "Smerling contract, 1942," he announces.

Many of us are probably just as disorganized as Costello's "filing system," though I suspect more than a few (okay, me included) would contend that we *really can* find things in the clutter we like to call a desk. Whether we're kidding ourselves or not, becoming more organized in our lives—whether we're students, homebodies or career-ladder climbers—is key to succeeding at home, in school and on the job.

Self-quiz: How's your planning IQ?

To learn something about your present orientation to planning, take this quiz adapted from Jonathan and Susan Clark's *Make the Most of Your Workday* (Career Press, 1994), circling the answer that describes your orientation: (3) agree (2) not sure (1) disagree.

I take regular time for planning every day.	3 2 1
I have a personally chosen calendar or organizational system.	3 2 1
I prioritize all my assignments... daily.	3 2 1
I usually complete a Daily Schedule (see page 70).	3 2 1
I do not have difficulty making decisions.	3 2 1
I work daily on parts of projects due more than a week from now.	3 2 1
The gas tank in my car is presently at least half full.	3 2 1
I know exactly when my most productive time of day is.	3 2 1
I know my most important assignment for tomorrow.	3 2 1
I have a current Project Board (see page 64).	3 2 1

How did you do?

25 or more	You have a plan, and are working on it.
15 to 24	Sometimes your day gets the better of you.
less than 15	How you are holding up under this crisis?

Why things don't get done

Are you frustrated at the end of the day? Is your to-do list nearly as long at the end of the day as it was in the beginning? Do you sometimes feel you've spent all day spinning your wheels? Nearly all productivity problems can be traced to one or more of the items on the following list.

- **No clear goals.** Without a specific sense of purpose, it's impossible to effectively manage and organize your priorities. If you don't know where you're going, any road will take you there.

- **Lack of priorities.** The best to-do list ever written is useless if it hasn't been prioritized. Most people naturally work on the easy or fun things first. They may cross off a majority of their list, but miss the most important items!

- **No daily plan.** Beginning your day without a plan of action is a formula for spending all day doing the wrong things. It invites anyone and everyone to interrupt your activities. You will passively allow unwelcome intrusions, because you'll have no way to defend yourself.

- **Perfectionism.** Are you unable to complete and release an assignment (paper, lab report, presentation, whatever) until it is done perfectly? Can you still see ways for something to be done better? Even if you can't see anything, does it nag you that there must be *something* you overlooked?

- **Personal disorganization.** No matter how organized your priorities or how effective your daily plan, you may be losing irretrievable time searching for things that are lost in the messes on your desk, in your files, closets and even your car.

- **Interruptions.** Your day can be going according to schedule...until a friend drops in or a game of "Killer Frisbee" commences. Many of these occurrences can be eliminated; those that can't must be controlled.

- **Procrastination.** It always *seems* like a good idea to "Scarlett O'Hara" your schedule. After all, tomorrow *is* another day. But it catches up with you!

If some or all of these apply to you, it's time to change some habits. If you're resolved to do so, I have some great news: Not only can bad habits be broken, but they can be replaced by good habits relatively easily. In fact, it's much easier to replace a habit than to break it. Just replace the "slob habit" with the good organizational habits in this book. Here's your battle plan:

- **Begin today.** The best time to start working on your resolve to be better organized is *today*. Don't procrastinate. Your motivation and resolve will not be stronger in a month than they are now. Start now and set a goal to acquire this new habit in the next 30 days!

- **Spread the word.** Don't keep your resolve a secret. Commit yourself to positive change by telling your friends and family what you've decided to do and by challenging them to keep you to your commitment.

- **Practice, practice, practice.** Practice is the motor oil that lubricates any habit's engine. The more you do something, the more ingrained it becomes.

The goal pyramid

One way to visualize all your goals—and their relation to each other—is to construct what I call a *goal pyramid*. Here's how to do it:

1. Centered at the top of a piece of paper, write down what you hope to ultimately gain from your education. This is your long-range goal and the pinnacle of your pyramid.

2. Below your long-range goal(s), list mid-range goals—milestones or steps that will lead you to your eventual target.

3. Below the mid-range goals, list as many short-range goals as you can—smaller steps that can be completed in relatively short periods of time.

Change your goal pyramid as you progress through school. You may eventually decide on a different career. Or your mid-range goals may change as you decide on a different path leading to the long-range goal. The short-range goals will undoubtedly change, even daily.

The process of creating your own goal pyramid allows you to see *how* all those little daily and weekly steps you take can lead to your mid-range and long-term goals, and will thereby motivate you to work on your daily and weekly tasks with more energy and enthusiasm.

Make goal-setting a part of your life

The development of good study skills is the highway to your goals, whatever they are. No matter how hard you have to work or how much adversity you have to overcome along the way, the journey will indeed be worth it.

How do you make setting goals a part of your life? Here are some hints I think will help:

1. **Be realistic when you set goals.** Don't aim too high or too low and don't be particularly concerned when (not *if*) you have to make adjustments along the way.

2. **Be realistic about your expectations.** An improved understanding of a subject you have little aptitude for is preferable to getting hopelessly bogged down if total mastery of the subject is just not in the cards.

3. **Don't give up too easily.** You can be *overly* realistic—too ready to give up just because something is a trifle harder than you'd like. Don't aim too high and feel miserable when you don't come close, or aim too low and never achieve your potential—find the path that's right for you.

4. **Concentrate on areas that offer the best chance for improvement.** Unexpected successes can do wonders for your confidence and might make it possible for you to achieve more than you thought you could even in other areas.

5. **Monitor your achievements and keep resetting your goals.** Daily, weekly, monthly, yearly, ask yourself how you've done and where you'd like to go *now*.

How perfect are you?

What is a perfectionist and are you one? And if you are, why is it a problem? (If you answered no to the first two questions, you can freely skip this section. I suspect I'm speaking to a minority of my readers here.)

Perfectionists care perhaps *too* much, finding it impossible to be satisfied with anything less than "perfect" work (as they define it), presuming that such an ideal can actually be attained.

It is possible, of course, to score a "perfect" 100 on a test or to get an A+ on a paper the teacher calls "Perfect!" in the margin. But in reality, doing anything "perfectly" is an impossible task.

What does all this have to do with you? Nothing, unless you find yourself spending two hours polishing an already A+ paper or half an hour searching for that one "perfect" word or an hour rewriting great notes to make them "absolutely perfect." In other words, while striving for perfection may well be a noble trait, it can very easily, perhaps inevitably, become a major problem if it becomes an uncontrollable and unstoppable urge that seriously inhibits your enjoyment of your work and your life.

If you really would prefer spending another couple of hours polishing that A+ paper to taking in a movie, reading a book or getting some *other* assignment done, be my guest. Is the last 10 percent or so really worth it? In some cases it is, but not usually.

Three more rules to help you get organized

As you begin to make goal-setting and organization a part of your daily life, here are three concepts that will make a huge difference in your success:

Small changes, over time, make a big difference

A simple, tiny change in your behavior may have virtually negligible results, but make *hundreds* of small changes, and the effects can be earth-shattering!

Make this rule become an automatic part of your thought process and your actions. It will help you understand the often small difference between success and failure, productivity and frustration, happiness and agony. It's so simple it's deceptive. Maybe just a little more training. Maybe a slightly better method of planning. Maybe just one tiny habit overcome. Maybe all of these and more. Each one alone is almost inconsequential, but when added up, the advantage is incredible!

The 80-20 Rule (Pareto Principle)

Another rule that you can apply to make a difference in how well you organize and manage your priorities is the 80-20 Rule, also known as the Pareto Principle.

Victor Pareto was an Italian economist and sociologist at the turn of the 20th century who studied the ownership of land in Italy. Pareto discovered that more than 80 percent of all the land was owned by less than 20 percent of the people. As he studied other things that people owned (including money), he found the same principle held true: 20 percent or less of the people always ended up with 80 percent or more of whatever he measured.

The most astonishing revelation about the 80-20 Rule is its opposite side: If 20 percent of activities are producing 80 percent of the results, then the other 80 percent of activities are, in total, only giving 20 percent of the results.

Remember: To apply the 80-20 Rule to managing your priorities, remind yourself that 20 percent of the activities on your list are going to produce 80 percent of the results and payoff. Your question must constantly be, "Which activities are the 20-percenters?"

Take advantage of "in-between" time

You can be even more productive by identifying the little windows of opportunity that pass through your life each day. They don't arrive with much fanfare, so if you're not alert to them, they will sneak right past you. What must you do with this "in-between" time? Recognize it as soon as it occurs *and* utilize it immediately by taking a premeditated action. If you don't have a plan, you will waste this time!

Here are some suggestions:

- Make phone calls.
- Read something.
- Mail letters.
- Pick up groceries (or make your grocery list).
- Clean up your desk and return things to their proper places.
- Review your Daily Schedule and reprioritize, if necessary.
- Go through your mail.
- Write a quick note or letter home.
- Proofread some or all of one of your papers.
- Think! (About an upcoming assignment, a paper you're writing, etc.)
- Relax!

Chapter 3

Organize your studying

You *can* study smarter. You *can* put in less time and get better results. But learning how to do so *is* hard, because learning of *any* kind takes discipline. And learning self-discipline is, to many of us, the most difficult task of all.

If you're currently doing little or nothing in the way of schoolwork, then you *are* going to have to put in more time and effort. How much more? Or even more generally, how long should you study, period? Until you get the results you want to achieve.

The smarter you are and the more easily you learn and adapt the techniques in this book, the more likely you'll be spending less time on your homework than before. But the further you need to go—from Ds to As rather than from Bs to As—the more you need to learn and the longer you need to give yourself to learn it.

Don't get discouraged. You will see results surprisingly quickly.

Get ready for a lifelong journey

Learning how to study is really a long-term process. Once you undertake the journey, you will be surprised at the number of landmarks, pathways, side streets and road signs you'll find. Even after you've transformed yourself into a better student than you'd ever hoped to be, you'll inevitably find one more signpost that offers new information, one more pathway that leads you in an interesting new direction.

Consider learning how to study a *lifelong process* and be ready to modify anything you're doing as you learn other methods.

This is especially important right from the start when you consider your overall study strategies. How long you study per night, how long you work on a particular subject and how often you schedule breaks are going to vary considerably depending on how well you were doing before you read this book, how far you have to go, how interested you are in getting there, how involved you are in other activities, the time of day, your general health, etc. Are you getting the idea?

It gets more complicated: What's your study sequence? Hardest assignments first? Easiest? Longest? Shortest? Are you comfortable switching back and forth from one to another or do you prefer to focus on a single assignment from start to finish?

This gets even more difficult when you consider that the tasks themselves may have a great effect on your schedule. Fifteen-minute study unit increments might work well for you most of the time (though I suspect half an hour is an ideal unit for most of you, an hour only for those of you who can work that long without a break and who have assignments that traditionally take that long to complete).

On the other hand, you may have no problem at all working on a long project in fits and starts, 15 or 20 minutes at a time, without needing to retrace your steps each time you pick it up again.

What's the lesson in all of this? There is no ideal, no answer, certainly no "right" answer, to many of the questions I've posed. It's a message you'll read in these pages over and over again: Figure out what works for you and keep on doing it. If it later stops working or doesn't seem to be working as well, change it.

None of the organizational techniques discussed at length in this book is carved in stone. You not only should feel free to adapt and shape and bend them to your own needs, you *must* do so.

Creating your study environment

On page 48, I have included a checklist for you to rate your study environment. It includes not just *where* you study—at home, in the library, at a friend's—but when and *how* you study, too. Once you've identified what works for you, avoid those situations in which you *know* you don't perform best. If you don't know the answer to one or more of the questions, take the time to experiment.

Study groups: What are friends for?

I was 35 years old and a devoted watcher of the television show *The Paper Chase* before I was introduced to the concept of a study group. This series was supposed to be about a law school that seemed just this side of hell, so sharing the load with other students wasn't just a good idea, it was virtually mandatory. My high school wasn't hell, not even a mild purgatory, but I still think a study group would have been beneficial. If I had thought of the idea I would have probably started one.

My Ideal Study Environment

How I receive information best:

1. ❑ Orally ❑ Visually

In the classroom, I should:

2. ❑ Concentrate on taking notes ❑ Concentrate on listening

3. ❑ Sit in front ❑ Sit in back ❑ Sit near window or door

Where I study best:

4. ❑ At home ❑ In the library ❑ Somewhere else:
   _____

When I study best:

5. ❑ Every night; little on weekends ❑ Mainly on weekends
   ❑ Spread out over seven days

6. ❑ In the morning ❑ Evening ❑ Afternoon

7. ❑ Before dinner ❑ After dinner

How I study best:

8. ❑ Alone ❑ With a friend ❑ In a group

9. ❑ Under time pressure ❑ Before I know I have to

10. ❑ With music ❑ In front of TV ❑ In a quiet room

11. ❑ Organizing an entire night's studying before I start
    ❑ Tackling and completing one subject at a time

I need to take a break:

12. ❑ Every 30 minutes or so ❑ Every hour
    ❑ Every 2 hours ❑ Every ____ hours

The idea is simple: Find a small group of like-minded students and share notes, question each other, prepare for tests together. To be effective, obviously, the students you pick to be in your group should share all, or at least most, of your classes.

Even if you find only one or two other students willing to work with you, such cooperation will be invaluable, especially in preparing for major exams.

Tips for forming your own study group

- I suggest four students minimum, probably six maximum. You want to ensure everyone gets a chance to participate while maximizing the collective knowledge and wisdom of the group.

- While group members needn't be best friends, they shouldn't be overtly hostile to one another, either. Seek diversity of experience, demand common dedication.

- Try to select students who are at least as smart, committed and serious as you. That will encourage you to keep up and challenge you a bit. Avoid a group in which you're the "star"—at least until you flicker out during the first exam.

- Avoid inviting members who are inherently unequal—boyfriend/girlfriend combinations, in which one may be inhibited by their *amore*'s presence; situations where one student works for another; situations where underclassmen and upperclassmen may stifle one another, etc.

- Decide early on if you're forming a study group or a social group. If the latter, don't pretend it's the former. If the former, don't just invite your friends and sit around discussing your teachers.

- There are a number of ways to organize. My suggestion is to assign each class to one student. That student must master that assigned class, doing, in addition to the usual assignments, any extra reading (recommended by the professor or not) necessary to achieve that goal, taking outstanding notes, outlining the course (if the group so desires), being available for questions and preparing various practice quizzes, midterms and finals as needed, to help test the other students' mastery.

  Needless to say, all of the other students attend all classes, take their own notes, do their own reading and homework assignments. But the student assigned that class attempts to learn as much as the professor, to actually be the "substitute professor" of that class in the study group. (So if you have five classes, a five-person study group is ideal.)

- Make meeting times and assignments formal and rigorous. Consider establishing rigid rules of conduct. Better to shake out the nonserious students early. You don't want anyone who is working as little as possible but hoping to take advantage of *your* hard work.

- Consider appointing a chair (rotating weekly, if you wish) in charge of keeping everyone on schedule and settling disputes before they disrupt the study group.

- However you organize, clearly decide—early—the exact requirements and assignments of each student. Again, you never want the feeling to emerge that one or two of you are trying to "ride the coattails" of the others.

Where should you study?

1. **At the library.** There may be numerous choices, from the large reading room, to quieter, sometimes deserted specialty rooms, to your own, solitary study cubicle. My favorite "home away from home" at Princeton was a little room that seemingly only four or five of us knew about—with four wonderfully comfortable chairs, subdued lighting, phonographs with earplugs and a selection of some 500 classical records. For someone like me, who requires music to study, it was a custom-made study haven!

2. **At home.** Remember that this is the place where distractions are most likely to occur. No one tends to telephone you at the library, and little brothers (or your own kids) will not find you easily in the "stacks." It is, of course, usually the most convenient place to make your study headquarters. It may not, however, be the most effective.

3. **At a friend's, neighbor's or relative's.** This may not be an option at all for most of you, even on an occasional basis, but you still may want to set up one or two alternative study sites. Despite many experts' opinion that you must study in the same place every night (with which I don't agree, by the way), I have a friend who simply craves some variety to help motivate him. He has four different places in which he likes to study and he simply rotates them from night to night. Do whatever you find works best for you.

4. **In an empty classroom.** Certainly an option at many colleges and perhaps some private high schools, it is an interesting idea mainly because so few students have ever thought of it! While not a likely option at a public high school, it never hurts to ask if you can't make some arrangements. Since many athletic teams practice until 6 p.m. or later, even on the high school level, there may be a part of the school open—and usable with permission—even if the rest is locked up tight.

5. **At your job.** Whether you're a student working part-time or a full-time worker going to school part-time, you may be able to make arrangements to use an empty office, even during regular office hours, or perhaps after everyone has left (depending on how much your boss trusts you). If you're in junior high or high school and a parent, friend or relative works nearby, you may be able to work from just after school until closing time at that person's workplace.

When should you study

As much as possible, create a routine time of day for your studying. Some experts contend that doing the same *thing* at the same *time* every day is the most effective way to organize any ongoing task. Some students find it easier to set aside specific blocks of time during the day, each day, in which they plan on studying.

No matter who you are, the time of day you'll study is determined by these factors:

1. **Study when you're at your best.** What is your peak performance period—the time of day you do your best work? This period varies from person to person—you may be dead to the world until noon but able to study well into the night, or up and alert at the crack of dawn but distracted and tired if you try to burn the midnight oil.

2. **Consider your sleep habits.** Habit is a very powerful influence. If you always set your alarm for 7 a.m., you may find that you wake up then even when you forget to set it. If you have grown accustomed to going to sleep around 11 p.m., you will undoubtedly become quite tired if you try to stay up studying until 2 a.m., and probably accomplish very little in those three extra hours.

3. **Study when you can.** Although you want to sit down to study when you are mentally most alert, external factors also play a role in deciding when you study. Being at your best is a great goal but not always possible: Study whenever circumstances allow.

4. **Consider the complexity of the assignment when you allocate time.** The tasks themselves may have a great effect on your schedule. Don't schedule one hour for an 80-page reading assignment when you know you read half a page per minute...on a good day.

Evaluate your study area

Whatever location you choose as your study base, how you set up your study area can affect your ability to stay focused and, if you aren't careful, seriously inhibit quality study time. Sit down at your desk or study area right now and evaluate your own study environment:

1. Do you have one or two special places reserved just for studying? Or do you study wherever seems convenient or available at the time?

2. Is your study area a pleasant place? Would you offer it to a friend as a good place to study? Or do you dread it because it's so depressing?

3. How's the lighting? Is it too dim or too bright? Is the whole desk well lit? Or only portions of it?

4. Are all the materials you need handy?

5. What else do you do here? Do you eat? Sleep? Write letters? Read for pleasure? If you try to study at the same place you sit to listen to your music or chat on the phone, you may find yourself doing one when you think you're doing the other!

6. Is your study area in a high-traffic or low-traffic area? How often are you interrupted by people passing through?

7. Can you close the door to the room to avoid disturbances and outside noise?

8. When do you spend the most time here? What time of day do you study? Is it when you are at your best? Or do you inevitably study when you're tired and less productive?

9. Are your files, folders and other class materials organized and near the work area? Do you have some filing system in place for them?

Staying focused on your studies

If you find yourself doodling and dawdling more than reading and remembering, try these solutions:

1. **Create a work environment in which you're comfortable.** The size, style and placement of your desk, chair and lighting may all affect whether or not you're distracted from the work at hand. Take the time to design the area that's perfect for you.

2. **Turn up the lights.** Experiment with the placement and intensity of lighting in your study area until you find what works for you, both in terms of comfort and as a means of staying awake and focused.

3. **Set some rules.** Let family, relatives and especially friends know how important your studying is and that specific hours are inviolate.

4. **Take the breaks you need.** Don't just follow well-intentioned but bogus advice about how long you should study before taking a break. Break when *you* need to.

Fighting tiredness and boredom

You've chosen the best study spot and no one could fault you on its setup. You're still using pencils to prop up your eyelids? Help is on the way:

Take a nap. What a concept! When you're too tired to study, take a short nap to revive yourself. Maximize that nap's effect by keeping it short—20 minutes is ideal, 40 minutes absolute maximum. After that, you go into another phase of sleep and you may wake even more tired than before.

Have a drink. A little caffeine won't harm you—a cup of coffee or tea, a glass of soda. Just be careful not to mainline it—caffeine's "wake-up" properties seem to reverse when you reach a certain level, making you far more tired than you were!

Turn down the heat. You needn't build an igloo out back, but too warm a room will inevitably leave you dreaming of sugarplums...while your paper remains unwritten on your desk.

Shake a leg. Go for a walk, high step around the kitchen, do a few jumping jacks—even mild physical exertion will give you an immediate lift.

Change your study schedule. Presuming you have some choice here, find a way to study when *you* are normally more awake and/or most efficient.

Studying with small kids

So many more of you are going to school while raising a family, I want to give you some ideas that will help you cope with the Charge of the Preschool Light Brigade:

Plan activities to keep the kids occupied. The busier you are in school and/or at work, the more time your kids will want to spend with you when you *are* home. If you spend some time with them, it may be easier for them to play alone, especially if you've created projects *they* can work on while *you*'re working on your homework.

Make the kids part of your study routine. Kids love routine, so why not include them in yours? If 4 p.m. to 6 p.m. is always "Mommy's Study Time," they will soon get used to it, especially if you make spending other time with them a priority and if you take the time to give them something to do during those hours.

Use the television as a baby sitter. While many of you will have a problem with this—it's one that I and my 7-year-old deal with weekly, if not daily—it may be the lesser of two evils. And you can certainly rent (or tape) enough quality shows so you don't have to worry about the little darlings watching street gangs bash skulls (or bashing skulls themselves on some video game system).

Plan your study accordingly. Unless you are right up there in the Perfect Parent Pantheon, all these things will not keep your kids from interrupting every now and then. While you can minimize such intrusions, it's virtually impossible to eliminate them entirely. So don't try— plan your schedule *assuming* them. For one, that means taking more frequent breaks to spend five minutes with your kids. They'll be more likely to give you the 15 or 20 minutes at a time *you* need if they get periodic attention themselves.

Find help. Spouses can occasionally take the kids out for dinner and a movie (and trust me, the kids will encourage you to study *more* if you institute this!), relatives can baby-sit (at their homes) on a rotating basis, playmates can be invited over (allowing you to send your darling to their house the next day), you may be able to trade baby-sitting chores with other parents at school and professional day care may be available at your child's school or in someone's home for a couple of hours a day.

Finally, use the Pre-Test Organizer on pages 58 and 59 to figure out your plan of action for the next test.

You *can* be successful without killing yourself!

Pre-Test Organizer

Class:_____Teacher:_____

Test date:_____ Time: From_____ to_____

Place:_____

Special instructions to myself (e.g., take calculator, dictionary, etc.):_____

_____

Materials I need to study for this test (check all needed):

- ❏ Book
- ❏ Workbook
- ❏ Class notes
- ❏ Handouts
- ❏ Tapes/videos
- ❏ Old tests
- ❏ Other _____

Format of the test will be (write the number of T/F, essays, etc., and total points for each section):

_____

_____

_____

_____

_____

Study group meetings (times, places):

1. _____
2. _____
3. _____
4. _____
5. _____

Material to be covered:
Indicate topics, sources and amount of review (light or heavy) required. Check box when review is completed.

Topic	Sources	Review
_____	_____	☐ ____
_____	_____	☐ ____
_____	_____	☐ ____
_____	_____	☐ ____
_____	_____	☐ ____
_____	_____	☐ ____
_____	_____	☐ ____

After the test:
Grade I expected_____Grade I received_____
What did I do that helped me?_____
_____
_____
_____
_____
_____

What else should I have done?_____
_____
_____
_____
_____
_____
_____
_____

Chapter 4

Organize your months, weeks and days

Now you're ready to plan!

We'll begin by developing a time management plan for an entire term...before it begins, of course. This term plan will allow you to keep your sights on the "big picture." You'll see the forest, even when you're in the midst of the trees...and a majority of them are oversized redwoods.

By being able to take in your entire term—every major assignment, every test, every paper, every appointment—you will be less likely to get caught up spending more time on a lower-priority class, just because it requires regularly scheduled reports, while falling behind in a more important one, which only requires reading.

And when you can actually *see* you have a test in accounting the same week your zoology project is due, you can plan ahead and finish the project early. If you decide (for whatever reason) not to do so, at least you won't be caught by surprise when crunch time comes.

Start planning early

For your long-term planning to be effective, however, you must start early. Students who fail to plan *before* the school term begins often find themselves wasting time filling in their schedules one event at a time during the term. They may also find themselves feeling disorganized throughout the term. Starting early, on the other hand, increases your ability to follow a systematic plan of attack.

All college students—and some high school students—are able to pick and choose courses according to their own schedules, likes, dislikes, goals, etc. The headiness of such freedom should be tempered with the commonsense approach you're trying to develop through reading this book. Here are a few hints to help you along:

1. Whenever possible, consider each professor's reputation as you decide whether to select a particular course (especially if it is an overview or introductory course that is offered in two or three sessions). Word soon gets around as to which professors' lectures are stimulating and rewarding—an environment in which learning is a joy, even if it isn't a subject you like!

2. Attempt to select classes so that your schedule is balanced on a weekly and even a daily basis, though this will not always be possible or advisable. (Don't change your major just to fit your schedule!) Try to leave an open hour or half-hour between classes—it's ideal for review, post-class note-taking, quick trips to the library, etc.

3. Try to alternate challenging classes with those that come more easily to you. Studying is a process of positive reinforcement. You'll need encouragement along the way.

4. Avoid late-evening or early-morning classes, especially if such scheduling provides you with large gaps of "down time."

5. Set a personal study pace and follow it. Place yourself on a study diet, the key rule of which is: *Don't overeat.*

Identify the starting line

You can't race off to your ultimate goal until you figure out where *your* starting line is. So the first step necessary to overhaul your current routine is to *identify* that routine in detail. My suggestion is to chart, in 15-minute increments, how you spend every minute of every day *right now*. While a day or two might be sufficient for some of you, I recommend you chart your activities for an entire week, including the weekend.

This is especially important if, like many people, you have huge pockets of time that seemingly disappear, but in reality are devoted to things like "resting" after you wake up, putting on makeup or shaving, reading the paper, waiting for transportation or driving to and from school or work. Could you use an extra hour or two a day, either for studying or for fun? Make better use of such "dead" time and you'll find all the time you need.

For example, learn how to do multiple tasks at the same time. Listen to a book on tape while you're working around the house; practice vocabulary or math drills while you're driving; have your kids, parents or roommates quiz you for an upcoming test while you are doing the dishes, vacuuming or dusting; and always carry your calendar, notebook(s), pens and a textbook with you—you can get a phenomenal amount of reading or studying done while in line at the bank, in the library, at the supermarket or on a bus or train.

Strategy tip: Identify those items on your daily calendar, whatever their priority, that can be completed in 15 minutes or less. These are the ideal tasks to tackle at the launderette, while waiting for a librarian to locate a book you need or while standing in line anywhere.

Collect what you need

As you begin your planning session, make sure you have all the information and materials you need to make a quality plan. Gather your class syllabuses; work schedule; dates of important family events, vacations or trips, other personal commitments (doctor appointments, birthday parties, etc.); and a calendar of any extracurricular events in which you plan to participate.

Keeping track of your day-to-day activities—classes, appointments, regular daily homework assignments and daily or weekly quizzes—will be dealt with later in this chapter. For now, I want to talk about the projects—term papers, theses, studying for midterm and final exams, etc.— that require completion over a long period of time—weeks, maybe even months.

Creating your Project Board

There are two excellent tools you can use for your long-term planning. The first is a Project Board, which you can put on any blank wall or right above your desk.

It's not necessary for you to construct your own Project Board, though it is certainly the least expensive alternative. There are ready-made charts for professionals available in a variety of formats for your convenience, including magnetic and erasable. (Once again you're learning something that you can use throughout your entire life: Professionals call their Project Boards "flow charts.") Your local art supply, stationery or bookstore may have a selection of such items.

How does the Project Board work? It is just a variation on a typical calendar. You can set it up vertically, with the months running down the left-hand side and the projects across the top. Or you can certainly switch it around and have the dates across the top and the projects running vertically (in fact, that's the way a lot of the ready-made ones are sold). It all depends on the available space you have on your wall.

Using your Project Board

In the case of each project, there is a key preparatory step before you can use the chart: You have to break down each general assignment into its component parts, the specific tasks involved in any large project.

Also include on your Project Board time for studying for all your final exams. Cramming for tests doesn't work very well in the short term and doesn't work at all over the long term, so take my advice and make it a habit to review your class notes on each subject on a *weekly or monthly* basis.

As a result of this plan, you'll allocate little time to last-minute cramming or even studying for a specific final the week before it is given (just a couple of hours to go over any details you're still a little unsure of or spend on areas you think will be on the test). While others are burning the midnight oil in the library the night before each exam, you're getting a good night's sleep and will enter the tests refreshed, relaxed and confident. Seems like a better plan to me.

As a byproduct of this study schedule, by the way, you will find that salient facts and ideas will remain with you long after anybody is testing you on them.

Now that you have your Project Board, what do you do with it? Keep adding any and all other important projects throughout the term and continue to revise it according to actual time spent, as opposed to time allocated. Getting into this habit will make you more aware of how much time to allocate to future projects and make sure that the more you do so, the more accurate your estimates will be.

Using a Term Planning Calendar

The Term Planning Calendar, an example of which is shown on page 68, can be used in concert with or in place of the Project Board.

To use it with the Project Board, start by transferring all the information from the Project Board to your Term Planning Calendar. Then *add* your weekly class schedule, work schedule, family celebrations, vacations and trips, club meetings and extracurricular activities. *Everything.* The idea is to make sure your Calendar has *all* your scheduling information, while your Project Board contains just the briefest summary that you can ingest in a glance.

Leave your Project Board on your wall at home; carry your Term Planning Calendar with you. Whenever new projects, appointments, meetings, etc. are scheduled, add them immediately to your Calendar. Then transfer the steps involving major projects to your Project Board.

To use it in place of the Project Board, just don't make a Project Board. Put all the information—including the steps of all your projects and the approximate time you expect each to take—right on the Calendar.

It's up to you which way to go. Personally, I prefer using *both,* for one simple reason: I like being able to look at the wall and see the entire term *at a glance*. I find it much easier to see how everything "fits" together this way than by trying to "glance" at a dozen different weekly calendars or even three monthly ones.

The fat lady isn't singing yet

It's time to become even more organized. The Project Board and Term Planning Calendar have given you a good start by helping you schedule the entire term. Now it's time to learn about the tools that will help you organize your days and weeks.

For any time management system to work, it has to be used continually. Before you go on, make an appointment with yourself for the end of the week—Sunday night is perfect—to sit down and plan for the following week. You don't have to spend a *lot* of time—a half hour is probably all it will take to review your commitments for the week and schedule the necessary study time.

Despite its brevity, this may just be the best time you spend all week, because you will reap the benefits of it throughout the week and beyond!

Step 1: Make your "to-do" list

First, identify everything you need to do this week. Look at your Project Board and/or Term Planning Calendar to determine what tasks need to be completed this week for all of your major school projects. Add any additional tasks that must be done—from sending a birthday present to your sister to attending your monthly volunteer meeting to completing homework that may have just been assigned.

Once you have created your list, you can move on to the next step, putting your tasks in order of importance.

Term Planning Calendar

Fill in due dates for assignments and papers, dates of tests, and important non-academic activities and events

Month	Mon	Tue	Wed	Thu	Fri	Sat	Sun

Step 2: Prioritize your tasks

When you sit down to study without a plan, you just dive into the first project that comes to mind. The problem with this approach has been discussed earlier: There is no guarantee that the first thing that comes to mind will be the most important. The point of the weekly Priority Task Sheet is to help you arrange your tasks *in order of importance.* That way, even if you find yourself without enough time for *everything,* you can at least finish the most important assignments.

First, ask yourself this question, "If I only got a few things done this week, what would I want them to be?" Mark these high-priority tasks with an "H." After you have identified the "urgent" items, consider those tasks that are least important—items that could wait until the following week to be done, if necessary. (This may include tasks you consider very important but that don't have to be completed *this week.)* These are low-priority items, at least for this week—mark them with an "L."

All the other items fit somewhere between the critical tasks and the low-priority ones. Review the remaining items. If you're sure none of them are either "H" or "L," mark them with an "M," for middle priority.

Strategy tip: If you push aside the same low-priority item day after day, week after week, at some point you should just stop and decide whether it's something you need to do at all! This is a strategic way to make a task or problem "disappear." In the business world, some managers purposefully avoid confronting a number of problems, waiting to see if they will simply solve themselves through benign neglect. If it works in business, it can work in school.

A completed Priority Task Sheet is on page 74. A blank form you can photocopy is on page 76.

Step 3: Fill in your Daily Schedule

Before you start adding papers, projects, homework, study time, etc., to your calendar, fill in the "givens"—the time you need to sleep, eat, work and attend class. Even if your current routine consists of meals on the run and sleep whenever you find it, build the assumption *right into your schedule* that you are going to get eight hours of sleep and three decent meals a day. You may surprise yourself and find that there is still enough time to do everything you need. (Though all of us probably know someone who sleeps three hours a night, eats nothing but junk and still finds a way to get straight As, most experts would contend that regular, healthy eating and a decent sleep schedule are key attributes to any successful study system.)

Now you're ready to transfer the items on your Priority Task Sheet to your Daily Schedule forms. (See page 75 for a sample completed Daily Schedule, page 77 for a blank form you can photocopy.)

Put in the "H" items first, followed by the "M" items. Then, fit in as many of the "L" items that you still have room for. By following this procedure, you'll make sure you devote the amount of time needed for your most important priorities. You can schedule your most productive study time for your most important tasks, and plug in your lower priorities as they fit.

Your three-hour block of free time Wednesday afternoon? Schedule your "H"-priority research-gathering, and plan to start that psychology assignment, an "L" priority, between lunch and your 2 p.m. class Thursday.

Other considerations

Besides the importance of the task and the available time you have to complete it, other factors will determine how you fit your Daily Schedules together. Some factors will be beyond your control—work schedules, appointments with professors, counselors, doctors. But there are plenty of factors you *do* control and should consider as you put together your Daily Schedules each week.

Schedule enough time for each task—time to "warm up" and get the task accomplished, but, particularly when working on long-term projects, not so much time that you "burn out." Every individual is different, but most students study best for blocks of one and a half to three hours, depending on the subject.

Don't overdo it. Plan your study time in blocks, breaking up work time with short leisure activities. (It's helpful to add these to your schedule as well.) For example, you've set aside three hours on Wednesday afternoon for that research assignment. Schedule a 15-minute walk to the ice cream shop somewhere in the middle of that study block. You'll find that these breaks help you think more clearly and creatively when you get back to studying.

Even if you tend to like longer blocks of study time, be careful about scheduling study "marathons"—a six- or eight-hour stretch rather than a series of two-hour sessions. The longer the period you schedule, the more likely you'll have to fight the demons of procrastination. Convincing yourself that you are really studying your heart out, you'll also find it easier to justify time-wasting distractions, scheduling longer breaks and, before long, quitting before you should.

Use your Daily Schedule daily

Each night (or in the morning before the day begins) look at your schedule for the upcoming day. How much free time is there? Are there "surprise" tasks that are *not* on your schedule but need to be? Are there conflicts you were unaware of at the beginning of the week?

If you plan well at the beginning of the week, this shouldn't happen often. But it invariably does. Just as often, you'll discover a class is canceled or a meeting postponed, which leaves you with a schedule change. By checking your Daily Schedule *daily—either the night before or the first thing in the morning*—you'll be able to respond to these changes.

How do you know whether to enter an assignment on your Daily Schedule or put it on the Project Board first?

If it's a simple task *and* if it will definitely be accomplished within a week—read pages 201-274, study for quiz, meet to discuss cheerleading tryouts with faculty—put it on the appropriate Daily Schedule Sheet(s).

If, however, it's a task that is complicated—requiring further breakdown into specific steps—and/or one that will require more than a week to complete, it should be "flow charted" on your Project Board. *Then* the individual steps should be added to your Daily Schedules. (I like to plan everything out the night before. It's a fantastic feeling to wake up and start the day completely organized.)

The most important 15 minutes of your day

Set aside 15 minutes every day to go over your daily and weekly priorities. While many businesspeople like to make this the first 15 minutes of their day, I recommend making it the last 15 minutes of your day. Why? Three great reasons:

1. **Your ideas will be fresher.** It's easier to analyze at the end of the day what you've accomplished...and haven't.

2. **It's a great way to end the day.** Even if your "study day" ends at 11 p.m., you'll feel fully prepared for the next day and ready to relax, anxiety-free.

3. **You'll get off to a great start the next morning.** If you use the morning to plan, it's easy to turn a 15-minute planning session into an hour of aimless "thinking." While others are fumbling for a cup of coffee, you're off and running!

Priority Rating	Scheduled?	**Priority Tasks This Week** Week of 3/28 through 4/3
		Sociology Paper
H		— Library Search
M		— Outline
L		— Rough Draft
		Math Assignments
H		— Ch. 4
M		— Ch. 5
M		— study for test

Daily Schedule

date: **3/30**

Assignments Due

Bio. Lab work.
Math, Ch. 4

To Do/Errands

Call Erin – 871-4031
Books to library
☑ Bank
☐ Groceries
Drop by Jim's

Homework

1) Math Ch.5 1-9
2) Sociology paper
(rough draft)

Schedule

Time	
5	
6	
7	
8	
9	Biology
10	Sociology
11	
12	Lunch w/ Kim
1	read:
2	ch. 5 (soc.)
3	Math class
4	TRAVEL
5	
6	Math homework
7	work on paper
8	
9	
10	
11	
12	

Priority Rating	Scheduled?	Priority Tasks This Week
		Week of ░░░░░ through ░░░░░

Daily Schedule

date: [ ]

Assignments Due	Schedule
	5
	6
	7
	8
	9

To Do/Errands	
	10
	11
	12
	1
	2
	3
	4
	5

Homework	
	6
	7
	8
	9
	10
	11
	12

Chapter 5

Dealing with life's daily traumas

Your organizational plan should be simple. Why commit to another complicated project that demands your time and mental energies? Yet, no matter how basic and easy to use your program may be, this doesn't guarantee that you won't be plagued with a time-crunch problem from time to time.

As you try to implement these skills in your life, you are bound to have some glitches. Learn some problem-solving skills so these study roadblocks don't stop your progress completely.

If you run into a "wall" on your path to organizational success, the best solution is to find creative ways to get *around* it, rather than trying to crash your way *through* it.

Time flies when you're having fun...

...and sometimes even when you're *not*. No matter how hard you try to stick to your schedule, you find that your assignments always take a lot longer than you had planned.

You schedule an hour to do your economics homework, and it takes you twice that long. You plan an afternoon at the library for research, and it's closing time before you're ready to leave. It seems like you spend all your time studying—and you're *still* not getting it done.

Solutions: It's time for an attitude check. Are you being too much of a perfectionist? Is it taking you so long to read because you're trying to memorize every word? Make sure your expectations for yourself are realistic. And don't exaggerate the importance of lower-priority assignments.

Consider altering your behavior—with a little help from an alarm clock. If you've planned an hour for your reading assignment, set the clock to go off when you should have completed it. Then, *stop reading* and go on to the next assignment. If you're not done, reassure yourself that you can go back to it later. You'll probably become conditioned to complete your assignments more quickly, and you won't run the risk of leaving your other, perhaps more important, work unfinished.

"I'm allergic to my desk"

There's nothing wrong with your study area. It's in a quiet corner of the house with few distractions. All your materials are nearby, and the area is well-lit and well-ventilated. But...every time you sit down to study, you find yourself coming up with *any* excuse to leave. Unable to focus on any assignment, your mind would be wandering out the window if there were one in front of you.

Solution: It can happen. You set up the ideal study area, follow your time management system and stick to your schedule religiously. Your intentions are good, but, for some reason, it just doesn't work. Bad vibes, maybe.

What can you do?

Change your environment!

Just as you can condition yourself to study, you can also condition yourself *not* to study in a particular location. Stick to your schedule, but try another area—another floor in the library, or even a place that may not seem to be as conducive to quiet study. Maybe you're one of those people who needs a little music or activity in the background to concentrate.

If changing your environment doesn't help, consider altering your study behavior. Are you trying to study at a time of day when you have far too much pent-up energy? Maybe switching your study time earlier or later would help. Try taking a brisk walk or exercising before you begin studying.

Think about other behavior: Have you had several cups of coffee (or cans of soda) prior to your study period? Caffeine overdose—or too much sugar *and* caffeine—could make it very difficult to concentrate.

A conspiracy to keep you from studying

Friends and family call when you're studying because they know that's the best time to reach you at home. Or you're interrupted by phone calls for family members or roommates. Worse yet are the calls from people taking surveys, asking for donations or trying to sell you something.

Solutions: A ringing phone is virtually impossible to ignore. Even if you're determined not to pick it up, it still demands your attention. A phone-answering machine will eliminate your getting roped into lengthy conversations, but your train of thought will still be interrupted.

There are a few environment-altering solutions: Turn off the ringer or unplug the phone and let your answering machine take calls while you're studying. Or remove yourself from within hearing distance—go to the library.

A little help from your "friends"

Your roommate, whose study hours differ from yours, always seems to want to spend "quality bonding time" in the middle of your heavy-duty reading assignments.

Solutions: It's not rude to refuse to talk to someone while you're studying. But it often feels like that, and I'd rather feel guilty about not studying than being rude to a friend. A favorite tip from human-relations specialists is to respond in a positive but diverting way—e.g., "It sounds like this is important to you. I really want to hear more. Can we talk in an hour when I'm done with this, so I can concentrate more on your problem?" (Granted, your roommate would look at you as if you were crazy if you talked like this. Put it in your own words—it's the attitude that's important.)

Another solution might be to put up a "Do Not Disturb" sign, indicating the time you will be available to talk. The visual signal helps remind others that you're busy before they unintentionally interrupt you with small talk.

You can't count on anyone

You painstakingly plan your schedule each week, religiously keeping track of each appointment, assignment and commitment you have. Unfortunately, others don't seem to have the same sense of responsibility you do. Your friends cancel social engagements, you arrive on time for a meeting and no one else in the group shows up, even your teacher postpones the pre-test study session.

Solution: Yes, its time for another attitude adjustment. Welcome to the real world!

First of all, there's really nothing you can do when someone else cancels or postpones a scheduled appointment. But if you remember, in the very first chapter of this book I said that fanaticism is not an element of a good time management program.

Occasional—and sometimes more than occasional—cancellations, postponements or reschedulings should *not* ruin your schedule.

Try looking at such last-minute changes as *opportunities*. Your doctor canceled your appointment? That means a free hour to get ahead in calculus, read your history, work out at the gym...or just do nothing!

Old habits die hard

As you begin to implement your own organizational system for success, you may need to rid yourself of some old habits:

1. **Don't make your schedule overly vague.** When you're scheduling your time, be specific about which tasks you plan to do, and when you plan to do them.

2. **Don't delay your planning.** It's easy to convince yourself that you will plan the details of a particular task when the time comes. But that way it's much too easy to forget your homework when your friends invite you to go to the park or out for a snack.

3. **Write *everything* down.** Not having to remember all these items will free up space in your brain for the things you need to concentrate on or *do* have to remember. As a general rule, write down the so-called little things and you'll avoid data overload and clutter.

4. **Learn to manage distractions.** "Don't respond to the urgent and forget the important." It's easy to become distracted when the phone rings, your baby brother chooses to trash your room or you realize your favorite TV show is coming on. But don't just drop your books and run off. Take a few seconds to make sure you have reached a logical stopping point.

5. **Don't "shotgun" plan.** Even if you haven't been following a systematic time management approach, you may have had some way of keeping important dates and events in mind. Some students use what might be called the "shotgun" approach—writing down assignments, dates and times on whatever is available. They wind up with so many slips of paper in so many places, their planning attempts are virtually worthless.

   Record all upcoming events and tasks on your Project Board and/or Term Planning Calendar. And always have your calendar with you so you can refer to it when you are planning a specific week or day or need to add an appointment or assignment to it.

6. **Don't "overschedule."** As you begin to follow a time management program, you may find yourself trying to schedule too *much* of your time. Once you get the "effectiveness bug" and become aware of how much you can accomplish, it might be tempting to squeeze more and more into your life.

7. **Be honest with yourself** when determining those things that require more effort, those that

come easier to you. Chances are you can't complete the outline for your term paper, study three chapters of biology and do your French assignment in the two hours you have between class and work. Schedule enough time to get each assignment done. Whenever possible, schedule pleasurable activities after study time, not before. They will act as incentives, not distractions.

8. **Remember that time is relative.** Car trips take longer if you have to schedule frequent stops for gas, food, necessities, etc., longer still if you start out during rush hour. Likewise, libraries are more crowded at certain times of the day or year, which will effect how fast you can get books you need, etc. So take the time of day into account.

9. **Be prepared.** As assignments are entered on your calendar, make sure you also enter items needed for their completion—texts, other books you have to buy, borrow or get from the library, special materials, etc. There's nothing worse than sitting down to do that assignment you've put off until the last minute and realizing that though *you're* finally ready to get to work, your supplies *aren't*...and at 10 p.m., you don't have a lot of options!

10. **Be realistic.** Plan according to *your* schedule, *your* goals and *your* aptitudes, not some ephemeral "standard." Allocate the time you expect a project to take *you*, not the time it might take someone else, how long your teacher tells you it should take, etc.

11. **Be flexible, monitor and adjust.** No calendar is an island. Any new assignment will affect whatever you've already scheduled. If you have a reasonably light schedule when a new assignment suddenly appears, it can just be plugged right into your calendar and finished as scheduled. But if you've already planned virtually every hour for the next two weeks, *any* addition may force you to change a whole day's plan. Be flexible and be ready. It'll happen.

12. **Look for more time savings.** If you find that you are consistently allotting more time than necessary to a specific chore—giving yourself one hour to review your English notes every Sunday but always finishing in 45 minutes or less—change your future schedule accordingly.

13. **Accomplish one task before going on to the next one**—don't skip around.

14. **Do your least favorite chores** (study assignments, projects, whatever) first—you'll feel better having gotten them out of the way!

15. **Try anything that works.** You may decide that color coding your calendar—red for assignments that must be accomplished that week, blue for steps in longer-term projects (which give you more flexibility), yellow for personal time and appointments, green for classes, etc.—makes it easier for you to tell at a glance what you need to do and when you need to do it.

16. **Adapt these tools to your own use.** Try anything you think may work—use it if it does, discard it if it doesn't.

There are thinkers and there are doers.

And there are those who think a lot about doing.

Organizing your life requires you to actually *use* the Project Board, Term Calendar, Priority Task Sheets and Daily Schedules we've discussed, not just waste more time "planning" instead of studying!

Planning is an ongoing learning process. Dive in and plan for your upcoming school term. Or if you're in the middle of a term now, plan the remainder of it right now. As you use your plan in the upcoming weeks and months, you will come up with new ideas for improving your time management system in the future and tailoring it to your own needs.

Chapter 6

Get organized for class

The pitfalls of poor note-taking skills

Most students take too many notes or too few.

Many of you will develop severe cases of carpal-tunnel syndrome in crazed efforts to reproduce every single word your teachers utter.

Others take notes so sparse that when reviewed weeks— or merely hours—later, they'll make so little sense that they might as well have been etched in Sanskrit.

If you feel compelled to take down your teacher's every pearly word, or recopy your entire text, you certainly won't have much of a social life—where would you ever find the time? Maybe you're so horrified at the prospect of *reliving* those hours of lectures and chapters of text that you simply *never* review your notes. And if you skip note-taking altogether...well, I don't need to tell you what kind of grades you should expect.

Note-taking should be the ultimate exercise in good old American pragmatism. Take notes only on the material that helps you develop a thorough understanding of your subject...and get good grades. And you should do it in a way that is, first and foremost, useful and understandable to *you*. A method that's easy to use would be a real plus.

Most students have a difficult time developing a good note-taking technique and recognizing the information that always shows up on tests—an understanding of which is essential for good grades.

Failing to learn good note-taking methods, they resort to what *I* think are useless substitutes, such as tape recorders and photocopying machines.

Know your teacher

First and foremost, you must know and understand the kind of teacher you've got and his or her likes, dislikes, preferences, style and what he or she expects you to get out of the class. Depending on your analysis of your teacher's habits, goals and tendencies, preparation may vary quite a bit, whatever the chosen format.

Take something as simple as asking questions during class, which I encourage you to do whenever you don't understand a key point. Some teachers are very confident fielding questions at any time during a lesson; others prefer questions to be held until the end of the day's lesson; still others discourage questions (or any interaction for that matter) entirely. Learn when and how your teacher likes to field questions and ask them accordingly.

No matter how ready a class is to enter into a free-wheeling discussion, some teachers fear losing control and veering away from their very specific lesson plan. Such teachers may well encourage discussion but always try to steer it into a predetermined path (their lesson plan). Other teachers thrive on chaos, in which case you can never be sure what's going to happen.

Approaching a class with the former teacher should lead you to participate as much as possible in the class discussion, but warn you to stay within whatever boundaries he or she has obviously set.

Getting ready for a class taught by the latter kind of teacher requires much more than just reading the text—there will be a lot of emphasis on your understanding key concepts, interpretation, analysis and your ability to apply those lessons to cases never mentioned in your text at all!

In general, here's how you should plan to prepare for any class before you walk through the door and take your seat:

Complete all assignments

Regardless of a particular teacher's style or the classroom format he or she is using, virtually every course you take will have a formal text (or two or three or more) assigned to it. Though the way the text explains or covers particular topics may differ substantially from your teacher's approach to the same material, your text is still the basis of the course and a key ingredient in your studying. You *must* read it, plus any other assigned books, *before* you get to class.

You may sometimes feel you can get away without reading assigned books beforehand, especially in a lecture format where you *know* the chance of being called on is slim to none. But fear of being questioned on the material is certainly not the only reason I stress reading the material that's been assigned. You will be lost if the professor decides—for the first time ever!—to spend the entire period asking *the students* questions. I've had it happen. And it was *not* a pleasant experience for the unprepared.

You'll also find it harder to take clear and concise notes because you won't know what's in the text (in which case you'll be frantically taking notes on material you could have underlined in your books the night before) or be able to evaluate the relative importance of the teacher's remarks.

Remember: Completing your reading assignment includes not just reading the *main* text but any *other* books or articles previously assigned, plus handouts that may have been previously passed out. It also means completing any nonreading assignments—turning in a lab report, preparing a list of topics or being ready to present your oral report.

Review your notes

Both from your reading and from the previous class. Your teacher is probably going to start this lecture or discussion from the point he or she left off last time. And you probably won't remember where that point was from week to week...unless you check your notes.

Have questions ready

Go over your questions before class. That way, you'll be able to check off the ones the lecturer or teacher answers along the way and only ask those left unanswered.

Prepare required materials

Including your notebook, text, pens or pencils and other such basics, plus particular class requirements like a calculator, drawing paper or other books.

Learn "selective" listening

Taking concise, clear notes is first and foremost the practice of discrimination—developing your ability to separate the essential from the superfluous, key concepts, key facts, key ideas from all the rest. In turn, this requires the ability to listen to what your teacher is saying and copying down only what you need to in order to understand the concept. For some, that could mean a single sentence. For others, a detailed example will be the key.

Just remember: The quality of your notes usually has little to do with their *length*—three key lines that reveal the core concepts of a whole lecture are far more valuable than paragraphs of less important data.

So why do some people keep trying to take verbatim notes, convinced that the more pages they cover with scribbles the better students they're being? It's probably a sign of insecurity—they haven't read the material and/or don't have a clue about what's being discussed, but at least they'll have complete notes!

Even if you find yourself wandering helplessly in the lecturer's wake, so unsure of what she's saying that you can't begin to separate the important, noteworthy material from the nonessential verbiage, use the techniques discussed in this book to organize and condense your notes anyway.

If you really find yourself so lost that you are just wasting your time, consider adding a review session to your schedule (to read or reread the appropriate texts) and, if the lecture or class is available again at another time, attend again. Yes it *is*, strictly speaking, a waste of your precious study time, but *not* if it's the only way to learn and understand important material.

Take notes on what you don't know

You *know* the first line of the Gettysburg Address. You *know* the chemical formula for water. You *know* what date Pearl Harbor was bombed. So why waste time and space writing them down?

Frequently, your teachers will present material you already know in order to set the stage for further discussion or to introduce material that is more difficult. Don't be so conditioned to automatically copy down dates, vocabulary, terms, formulas and names that you mindlessly take notes on information you already know. You'll just be wasting your time—both in class and later, when you review your overly detailed notes.

This is why some experts recommend that you bring your notes or outline of your textbook reading to class and *add your class notes to them.* I think it's an effective way to easily organize all your notes for that class, even if it effectively kills the idea of highlighting or underlining your text.

Observe your instructor's style

All instructors (perhaps I should say all *effective* instructors) develop a plan of attack for each class. They decide what points they will make, how much time they will spend reviewing assignments and previous lessons, what texts they will refer to, what anecdotes they will bring into the lecture to provide comic relief or human interest and how much time they'll allow for questions.

Building a note-taking strategy around each instructor's typical plan of attack for lectures is another key to academic success.

Throughout junior high school and much of high school, I had to struggle to get good grades. I took copious notes, studied them every night and pored over them before every quiz and exam.

I was rewarded for my efforts with straight As, but resented the hours I had to put in while my less ambitious buddies found more intriguing ways to spend their time.

But some of the brighter kids had leisure time, too. When I asked them how they did it, they shrugged their shoulders and said they didn't know.

These students had an innate talent that they couldn't explain, a sixth sense about what to study, what were the most important things a teacher said and what instructors were most likely to ask about on tests.

In fact, when I was in a study group with some of these students, they would say, "Don't worry, she'll never ask about that." And sure enough, she never did.

What's more, these students had forgotten many of the details I was sweating. They hadn't even bothered to write any of them down, let alone try to remember them.

What these students innately knew was that items discussed during any lesson could be grouped into several categories, which varied in importance:

- Information not contained in the class texts and other assigned readings.

- Explanations of obscure material covered in the texts and readings but with which students might have difficulty.

- Demonstrations or examples that provided greater understanding of the subject matter.

- Background information that put the course material in context.

As you are listening to an instructor, decide which of these categories best fits the information being presented to you. This will help you determine how detailed your notes on the material should be. (This will become especially easy as some time passes and you get to know the instructor.)

Read, read, read

Most good instructors will follow a text they've selected for the course. Likewise, unless they've written the textbook themselves (which you will find surprisingly common in college), most teachers will supplement it with additional information. Good teachers will look for shortcomings in textbooks and spend varying amounts of class time filling in these gaps.

As a result, it makes sense to stay one step ahead of your instructors. Read ahead in your textbook so that, as an instructor is speaking, you know what part of the lesson you should write down and what parts of it are *already* written down in your textbook. Conversely, you'll immediately recognize the supplemental material on which you might need to take more detailed notes.

Will you be asked about this supplemental material on your exams?

Of course, if you ask your teacher that question, he'll probably say something like, "You are expected to know everything that's mentioned in this class." That's why it's best to pay attention (and not ask stupid questions you already know the answers to!).

You will quickly learn to tell from a teacher's body language what he considers important and what he considers tangential.

In addition, your experience with the teacher's exams and spot quizzes will give you a great deal of insight into what he or she considers most important.

Sit near the front of the room

Minimize distractions by sitting as close to the instructor as you can.

The farther you sit from the teacher, the more difficult it is to listen. Sitting toward the back of the room means more heads bobbing around in front of you, more students staring out the window—encouraging you to do the same.

Sitting up front has several benefits. You will make a terrific first impression on the instructor—you might very well be the only student sitting in the front row. He'll see immediately that you have come to class to listen and learn, not just take up space.

You'll be able to hear the instructor's voice, and the instructor will be able to hear *you* when you ask and answer questions.

Finally, being able to see the teacher clearly will help ensure that your eyes don't wander around the room and out the windows, taking your brain with them.

So, if you have the option of picking your desk in class, sit right down in front.

Avoid distracting classmates

The gum cracker. The doodler. The practical joker. The whisperer. Even the perfume sprayer. Your classmates may be wonderful friends, entertaining lunch companions and ultimate weekend party animals, but their quirks, idiosyncrasies and personal hygiene habits can prove distracting when you sit next to them in class.

Knuckle-cracking, giggling, whispering and note-passing are just some of the evils that can avert your attention in the middle of your math professor's discourse on quadratic equations. Avoid them.

Listen for verbal clues

Identifying noteworthy material means finding a way to separate the wheat—that which you *should* write down—from the chaff—that which you should *ignore*. How do you do that? By *listening* for verbal clues and *watching* for the nonverbal ones.

Certainly not all teachers will give you the clues you're seeking. But many will invariably signal important material in the way they present it—pausing (waiting for all the pens to rise), repeating the same point (perhaps even one already made and repeated in your textbook), slowing down their normally supersonic lecture speed, speaking more loudly (or more softly), even by simply stating, "I think the following is important."

There are also numerous words and phrases that should *signal* noteworthy material (and, at the same time, give you the clues you need to logically organize your notes): "First of all," "Most importantly," "Therefore," "As a result," "To summarize," "On the other hand," "On the contrary," "The following (number of) reasons (causes, effects, decisions, facts, etc.)."

Such words and phrases give you the clues to not just write down the material that follows, but also to put it in context—to make a list ("First," "The following reasons"); to establish a cause-and-effect relationship ("Therefore," "As a result"); to establish opposites or alternatives ("On the other hand," "On the contrary"); to signify a conclusion ("To summarize," "Therefore"); or to offer an explanation or definition.

Look for nonverbal clues

If the teacher begins looking at the window, or his eyes glaze over, he's sending you a clear signal: "Put your pen down. This isn't going to be on the test. (So don't take notes!)"

On the other hand, if she turns to write something on the blackboard, makes eye contact with several students and/or gestures dramatically, she's sending a clear signal about the importance of the point she's making.

Learn how to be a detective—don't overlook the clues.

Ask questions often

Being an active listener means asking *yourself* if you understand everything that has been discussed. If the answer is "no," you must ask the instructor questions at an appropriate time or write down the questions you need answered later in order to understand the subject fully.

To tape or not to tape

I am opposed to using a tape recorder in class as a substitute for an active brain for the following reasons:

- **It's time-consuming.** To be cynical, not only will you have to waste time sitting in class, you'll have to waste more time listening to that class *again*!

- **It's virtually useless for review.** Fast-forwarding and rewinding cassettes to find the salient points of a lecture is torture. During the hectic days before an exam, do you really want to waste time listening to a whole lecture when you could just reread your notes?

- **It offers no backup.** Only the most diligent students record *and* take notes. What happens if your tape recorder malfunctions? How useful will blank or distorted tapes be when it's review time?

- **It costs money.** Compare the price of blank paper and a pen to that of recorder, batteries and tapes. The cost of batteries *alone* should convince you that you're better off going the low-tech route.

- **You miss the "live" clues** we discussed earlier. When all you have is a tape, you don't see that flash in your teacher's eyes, passionate arm-flailing, stern set of the jaw, any and all of which scream, "Pay attention. This will be on your test!"

Create your own shorthand

You don't have to be a master of shorthand to stream-
line your note-taking. Here are five ways:

1. **Eliminate vowels.** As a sign that was
   ubiquitous in the New York City subways used
   to proclaim, "If u cn rd ths, u cn gt a gd jb." (If
   you can read this, you can get a good job.) And,
   we might add, "u cn b a btr stdnt."

2. **Use word beginnings** ("rep" for
   representative, "con" for congressperson) and
   other easy-to-remember abbreviations.

3. **Stop putting periods** after all abbreviations
   (they add up!)

4. **Create your own symbols** and abbreviations
   based on your needs and comfort level.
   There are two specific symbols I think you'll
   want to create—they'll be needed again and again:

   Ⓦ That's my symbol for "What?" as in "What
   the heck does that mean?" "What did she
   say?" or "What happened? I'm completely
   lost!" It denotes something that's been
   missed—leave space in your notes to fill in
   the missing part of the puzzle after class.

   Ⓜ That's my symbol for "My thought." I want
   to separate my thoughts during a lecture
   from the professor's—put too many of your
   own ideas (without noting they're *yours*)
   and your notes begin to lose serious value!

5. **Use standard symbols** in place of words. The
   following list may help you. You may also
   recognize some of these from math and logic:

≈	Approximately
w/	With
w/o	Without
wh/	Which
→	Resulting in
←	As a result of/consequence of
+	And or also
*	Most importantly
cf	Compare; in comparison; in relation to
ff	Following
<	Less than
>	More than
=	The same as
↑	Increasing
↓	Decreasing
esp	Especially
Δ	Change
⊂	It follows that
∴	Therefore
∵	Because

Feel free to use your own code for these two instances; you certainly don't have to use mine.

While I recommend using all the "common" symbols and abbreviations listed previously *all* the time, in *every* class, in order to maintain consistency, you may want to create specific symbols or abbreviations for each class. In chemistry, "TD" may stand for thermodynamics, "K" for the Kinetic Theory of Gases (don't mix it up with the "K" for Kelvin). In history, "GW" is the Father of our country, "ABE" is Mr. Honesty, "FR" could be French Revolution (or "freedom rider"), "IR" is the Industrial Revolution.

How do you keep everything straight? Create a list on the first page of that class's notebook or binder section for the abbreviations and symbols you intend to use regularly through the semester.

Expanding on your "shorthand"

Continue to abbreviate *more* as additional terms become readily recognizable—in that way, the speed and effectiveness of your note-taking will increase as the school year grinds on.

Many students are prone to write *big* when they are writing fast and to use only a portion of the width of their paper. I guess they figure that turning over pages quickly means they are taking great notes. All it really means is that they are taking notes that will be difficult to read or use when it's review time.

Force yourself to write small and take advantage of the entire width of your note paper. The less unnecessary movement the better.

What to do after class

As soon as possible after your class, review your notes, fill in the "blanks," mark down questions you need to research in your text or ask during the next class, and remember to mark any new assignments on your weekly calendar.

I tend to discourage recopying your notes as a general practice, since I believe it's more important to work on taking good notes the first time around and not wasting the time it takes to recopy. *But* if you tend to write fast and illegibly, it might also be a good time to rewrite your notes so they're readable, taking the opportunity to summarize as you go. The better your notes, the better your chance of capturing and recalling the pertinent material.

It is not easy for most high school students to do so, but in college, where you have a greater say in scheduling your classes, I recommend "one period on, one off"—an open period, even a half hour, after each class to review that class's notes and prepare for the next one.

If you find yourself unable to take full advantage of such in-between time, schedule as *little* time between classes as you can.

Are you among the missing?

Even if you diligently apply all of the tips in this chapter, it will all be moot if you regularly miss class. So don't! It's especially important to attend all classes near semester's end. Teachers sometimes use the last week to review the entire semester (what a great way to minimize your *own* review time!) and/or clarify specific topics he feels might still be fuzzy and/or answer questions. Students invariably ask about the final exam during this period, and some teachers virtually outline what's going to be on the test!

If you *must* miss a class, find that verbatim note-taker who hasn't followed my advice and borrow *her* notes. That way, *you* get to decide what's important enough to copy down. (Some professors might even lend you *their* notes. It's worth asking!)

Chapter 7

Organize your reading and writing

Taking *effective* notes from your texts should:

- *Help you recognize* the most important points of a text.
- *Make it easier* for you to understand those important points.
- Enhance your memory of the text.
- Provide a *highly efficient* way to study for your exams.

Go for the gold, ignore the pyrite

Step one in effective note-taking from texts is to write down the *principle* points the author is trying to make. These main ideas should be placed either in the left-hand margin of your note paper, or as headings. *Do not write complete sentences.*

Then, write down the most important details or examples the author uses to support each of these arguments. These details should be noted under their appropriate main idea. I suggest indenting them and writing each idea on a new line, one under the other. Again, *do not use complete sentences.* Include only enough details so that your notes are not "Greek to you" when you review them.

I'm sure it's abundantly clear to all of you that not many best-selling authors moonlight writing textbooks. Most of the tomes given to you in classes—even the ones for *literature* classes—are poorly written, badly organized cures for insomnia. Dull is the kindest word to describe all but a few of them.

That said, it's also clear that no matter how dull the prose, your job is to mine the important details from your textbooks so you get good grades. Lest you have to wade through that lifeless mass of words more than once, why not take great notes the *first* time through?

You can borrow many of the strategies you implement for taking notes in class for your attack on your reading assignments. Just as you use your active brain to listen carefully to what your teacher talks about, you can use that same piece of equipment to *read* actively:

- Read, then write.

- Make sure you understand the big picture.

- Take notes on what you don't know.

These same principles we discussed in conjunction with taking notes in class apply to taking notes on your reading materials. But there are some additional strategies you should also consider.

Change the way you read

When we read books for pleasure, we tend to read, naturally, from beginning to the end. (Though some of us may be guilty of taking a peek at the last chapter of a suspenseful mystery novel.) Yet this linear approach, beginning at point A and moving in a direct manner to point B, is not necessarily the most effective way to read texts for information.

If you find yourself plowing diligently through your texts without having the faintest clue as to what you've read, it's time to change the way you read. The best students don't wade through each chapter of their textbooks from beginning to end. Instead, they read in an almost circular fashion. Here's how:

Look for clues

If we're curled up with the latest Stephen King thriller, we fully expect some clues along the way that will hint at the gory horror to come. And we count on Agatha Christie to subtly sprinkle keys to her mysteries' solutions long before they are resolved in the drawing room.

But most of you probably never tried to solve the mysteries of your own textbooks by using the telltale signs and signals almost all of them contain. That's right, *textbooks are riddled with clues* that will reveal to the perceptive student all the noteworthy material that must be captured. Here's where to find them:

Chapter heads and subheads. Bold-faced headings and subheadings announce the detail about the main topic. And, in some textbooks, paragraph headings or bold-faced lead-ins announce that the author is about to provide finer details. So start each reading assignment by going through the chapter, beginning to end, *reading only the bold-faced heads and subheads.*

Knowing what the author is driving at in a textbook will help you look for the important building blocks for her conclusions while you're reading. While it may not be as much fun to read a mystery novel this way, when it comes to textbook reading and note-taking, it will make you a much more *active* reader, and, consequently, make it much less likely that you will doze off while being beaten senseless by the usual ponderous prose.

Pictures, graphs and charts. Most textbooks, particularly those in the sciences, will have charts, graphs, numerical tables, maps and other illustrations. All too many students see these as mere fillers—padding to glance at, then forget.

If you're giving these charts and graphs short shrift, you're really shortchanging *yourself.* You don't have to redraw the tables in your notes, but observe how they supplement the text and what points they emphasize, and make note of these. This will help you put them into your own words, which will help you remember them later. And it will ensure that you don't have to continually refer to your textbooks when brushing up for an exam.

Highlighted terms, vocabulary and other facts. In some textbooks, you'll discover that key terms and other such information are highlighted within the body text. (And I *don't* mean by a previous student; consider such yellow-swathed passages with caution—their value is directly proportional to that student's final grade, which you don't know.) Whether boldface, italic or boxed, this is usually an indication that the material is noteworthy.

Questions. Some textbook publishers use a format in which key points are emphasized by questions, either within the body of the text or at the end of the chapter. If you read these questions *before* reading the chapter, you'll have a better idea of what material you need to pay closer attention to.

These standard organizational tools should make your reading job simpler. The next time you have to read a history, geography or similar text, try skimming the assigned pages first. Read the heads, the subheads and the callouts. Read the first sentence of each paragraph. Then go back and start reading the details.

To summarize the skimming process:

1. Read and be sure you understand the title or heading. Try rephrasing it as a question for further clarification of what you will read.

2. Examine all the subheadings, illustrations and graphics—these will help you identify the significant matter within the text.

3. Read *thoroughly* the introductory paragraphs, the summary and any questions at chapter's end.

4. Read the first sentence of every paragraph—this generally includes the main idea.

5. Evaluate what you have gained from this process: Can you answer the questions at the end of the chapter? Can you intelligently participate in a class discussion of the material?

6. Write a brief summary that capsulizes what you have learned from your skimming.

7. Based on this evaluation, decide whether a more thorough reading is required.

Now for the fine print

Now that you have gotten a good overview of the contents by reading the heads and subheads, reviewing the summary, picking up on the highlighted words and information and considering the review questions that may be included, you're finally ready to read the chapter.

If a more thorough reading is then required, turn back to the beginning. *Read one section (chapter, etc.) at a time.* And do not go on to the next until you've completed the following exercise:

1. Write definitions of any key terms you feel are essential to understanding the topic.

2. Write questions and answers you feel clarify the topic.

3. Write any questions for which you *don't* have answers—then make sure you find them through rereading, further research or asking another student or your teacher.

4. Even if you still have unanswered questions, move on to the next section and complete numbers one to three for that section. (And so on, until your reading assignment is complete.)

See if this method doesn't help you get a better handle on any assignment right from the start.

Because you did a preliminary review first, you'll find that your reading will go much faster.

*But...*don't assume that now you can speed through your reading assignment. Don't rush through your textbook, or you'll just have to read it again.

Sure, we've all heard about the boy and girl wonders who can whip through 1,000 or even 2,000 words per minute and retain everything, but most of us never will read that fast. That's fine—it's better to read something slowly and *remember* it than rush it into oblivion. Many great students—even those in law school or taking umpteen courses on the 19th-century novel—never achieve reading speeds even close to 1,000 words per minute. Some of them have to read passages they don't understand again and again to get the point. *There's nothing wrong with that.*

The most intelligent way to read is with comprehension, not speed, as your primary goal.

Many students underline in their textbooks or use magic markers to "highlight" them. This is a sure sign of masochism, as it guarantees only one thing: They will have to read a great deal of the deadly book again when they review for their exams.

Others write notes in the margin. This is a little bit better as a strategy for getting higher grades, but marginalia usually make the most sense only in context, so this messy method also forces the student to reread a great deal of text.

What's *the* most effective way to read and remember your textbooks?

The importance of outlining

Outlining a textbook, article or other secondary source is a little bit like what the Japanese call "reverse engineering"—a way of developing a diagram for something so that you can see exactly how it's been put together. Seeing how published authors build their arguments and marshal their research will help you when it comes time to write your own papers.

Seeing that logic of construction will also help you a great deal in remembering the book—by putting the author's points down in *your* words, you will be building a way to retrieve the key points of the book more easily from your memory.

What's more, outlining will force you to distinguish the most important points from those of secondary importance, helping you build a true understanding of the topic.

Do like the Romans do

Standard outlines use Roman numerals (I, II, III, etc.), capital letters, Arabic numerals (1, 2, 3, 4, etc.), and lower-case letters and indentations to show relationship and importance of topics in the text. While you certainly don't have to use the Roman-numeral system, your outline should be organized in the following manner:

Title
Author

I. First important topic in the text
 A. First subtopic
  1. First subtopic of A
   a. First subtopic of 1
   b. Second subtopic of 1
  2. Second subtopic of A
II. The second important topic in the text

Get the idea? In a book, the Roman numerals would usually refer to chapters; the capital letters to subheadings; and the Arabic numbers and lower-case letters to blocks of paragraphs. In an article or single chapter, the Roman numbers would correspond to subheadings, capital letters to blocks of paragraphs, Arabic numerals to paragraphs and small letters to key sentences.

The discipline of creating outlines will help you zero in on the most important points an author is making and capture them, process them and, thereby, retain them.

Sometimes an author will put the major point of a paragraph in the first sentence. But just as often the main idea of a paragraph or section will follow some of these telltale words: "therefore," "because," "thus," "since," "as a result."

When we see these words we should identify the material they introduce as the major points in our outline. The material immediately preceding and following almost always will be in support of these major points. The outline is an extraordinary tool for organizing your thoughts and your time.

Create a timeline

I always found it frustrating to read textbooks in social studies. I'd go through chapters on France and the Far East, and have a fairly good understanding of those areas, but no idea where certain events stood in a global context. As more and more colleges add multicultural curricula, you may find it even more difficult to "connect" events in 17th-century France or 19th-century Africa with what was happening in the rest of the world (let alone the U.S.).

An excellent tool for overcoming that difficulty is a timeline that you can update periodically. It will help you visualize the chronology and remember the relationship of key world events.

A simple, abridged timeline of Charles Dickens's literary life would look like this (I suggest you create a horizontal timeline, but the layout of this book makes reproducing it that way difficult, so here's a vertical version):

1812	Birth
1836	First book published (*Sketches by Boz*)
1837	*Pickwick Papers*
1838	*Oliver Twist*
1850	*David Copperfield*
1853	*Bleak House*
1857	*Little Dorrit*
1861	*Great Expectations*
1870	Death

This makes it easy to see that he was born as the U.S. was entering the War of 1812 and died soon after the end of the Civil War. If you added other literary figures from the same period, you would not soon forget that Dickens, Dostoyevsky, Tolstoy, Kierkegaard, Ibsen, Noah Webster, Emerson, Longfellow, Melville and Hawthorne, among many others, were all literary contemporaries. Adding nonliterary events to your timeline would enable you to make connections between what was being written and what was going on in the United States, Britain, Europe, Africa, etc.

Draw a concept tree

Another terrific device for limiting the amount of verbiage in your notes and making them more memorable is the concept tree. Like a timeline, the concept tree is a visual representation of the relationship among several key facts. For instance, one might depict the categories and examples of musical instruments this way:

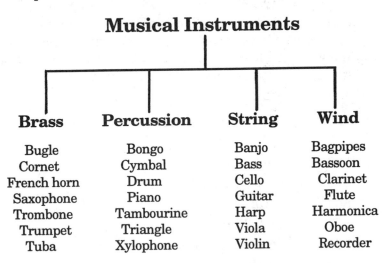

Musical Instruments

Brass	**Percussion**	**String**	**Wind**
Bugle	Bongo	Banjo	Bagpipes
Cornet	Cymbal	Bass	Bassoon
French horn	Drum	Cello	Clarinet
Saxophone	Piano	Guitar	Flute
Trombone	Tambourine	Harp	Harmonica
Trumpet	Triangle	Viola	Oboe
Tuba	Xylophone	Violin	Recorder

Now we can give credence to the old saying, "A picture is worth a thousand words," since timelines and concept trees will be much more helpful than mere words in remembering material, particularly conceptual. material. Developing them will ensure that your interest in the text will not flag too much.

Add a vocabulary list

Many questions on exams require students to define the terminology in a particular discipline. Your physics professor will want to know what vectors are, your calculus teacher will want to know about differential equations, your history professor will want you to be well-versed on the Cold War, and your English literature professor will require you to know about the romantic poets.

As you read your textbook, be sure to write down all new terms that seem important and their definitions. I used to draw a box around terms and definitions in my notes, because I knew these were among the most likely items to be asked about and the box would always draw my attention to them when I was reviewing.

Wait, you're not done yet

After you've finished taking notes on a chapter, go through them and identify the most important points, either with an asterisk or a highlighter. You'll probably end up marking about 40 to 50 percent of your entries. When you're reviewing for a test, you should read *all* of the notes, but your asterisks will indicate which points you considered the most important while the chapter was very fresh in your mind.

To summarize, when it comes to taking notes from your texts or other reading material, you should:

- Take a cursory look through the chapter before you begin reading. Look for subheads, highlighted terms and summaries at the end of the chapter to give you a sense of the content.

- Read each section thoroughly. While your review of the chapter "clues" will help you understand the material, you should read for comprehension rather than speed.

- Take notes immediately after you've finished reading, using mapping, the outline, timeline, concept tree and vocabulary list methods of organization as necessary.

- Mark with an asterisk or highlight the key points as you review your notes.

Notes on library materials

Sometime during your high school or college years, you will undoubtedly be called upon to do some extensive research, either for a term paper or some other major project. Such a task will indeed be a major undertaking. Note-taking will be only one aspect of the process, albeit an important one.

(While I will give you a terrific system for taking notes for a term paper or report in this chapter, I urge you to also read *Improve Your Writing*, which thoroughly covers *all* the important steps, from selecting a topic and developing an outline to researching and taking notes to writing, rewriting and proofreading your final paper.)

As you will discover, writing a term paper will require you to take notes from a number of sources, most of them available at the library. But the more periodicals, reference books and even microfiche you uncover as terrific sources of information for your project, the more likely you'll be told that you can't take these materials out of the library. You'll have to take your notes *at the library,* not at your leisure in the comfort of your room.

So you'll definitely want a note-taking system that is quick, thorough, efficient and precludes the necessity of having to return to the source *again*. What's the answer?

No, it's not photocopying.

Why photocopying is redundant

You've found a resource that's perfect for your term paper. Your first impulse might be to find the library photocopying machine and pump some quarters into it.

Is photocopying a help or a hindrance?

I used to employ a system of photocopying when preparing for my term papers. I would go to the library with nothing except a roll of dimes (photocopying was a lot cheaper in those days), and comb the card catalog, the stacks and the periodicals index for possible sources, using the library-supplied pencils to write the information down on call slips. I'd stack the volumes and periodicals around me at one of the tables and comb through them for hours, looking for juicy quotes and fun factoids.

I'd mark the books with those handy call slips. Then, I'd haul all of the useful sources over to the photocopier and begin Xeroxing away my hard-earned money.

I'd wind up going home with a pile of photocopies that I had to *reread*, which I'd do armed with pens of as many different colors as I could find. I'd underline all of the related passages with the same color, pick up another pen and go sifting through the photocopies again. This method certainly helped me produce some darned good papers, but it also ensured that I spent too much time rereading information, organizing and reorganizing the research before I ever began actually writing.

I'm about to save you a lot of grief by letting you in on one of the greatest card tricks you've ever seen. And, by the way, you won't ever have to wait in line for the photo-copying machine at the library again.

A great indexing system

Index cards will cut the time it takes to research and organize a term paper in half.

Here's how they work:

As you'll learn when you read *Improve Your Writing,* developing a preliminary outline is an important early step in the paper-writing process. Assuming you have completed this step, you would then be prepared to gather information for your term paper or research project. Proceed to your local stationery store and buy a supply of 3 x 5 note cards.

As you review each source, you'll discover some are packed with helpful information, while others may have no useful material at all. Once you determine that you will use a source, make a working bibliography card:

- **In the upper right-hand corner of the card**: Write the library call number (Dewey decimal or Library of Congress number), or any other detail that will help you locate the material ("Science Reading Room," "Main Stacks, 3rd Floor," etc.).

- **On the main part of the card**: Write the author's name, if one is given, last name first. Include the title of the article, if applicable, and write and underline the name of the book, magazine or other publication. Include any other details, such as date of publication, edition, volume number or page numbers where the article or information was found.

- **In the upper left-hand corner**: Number the card—the card for the first source you plan to use, for example, is #1, the second is #2 and so on. If you accidentally skip a number or end up not using a source for which you've filled out a card, don't worry. It's only important that you assign a different number to each card.

- **At the bottom of the card**: Write the name of the library (if you're researching at more than one) at which you found the source.

By filling out a card for each source, you have just created your *working bibliography*—a listing of all your sources that will be an invaluable tool when you have to prepare the final bibliography for your term paper.

Shuffling cards is a good deal

With index cards, you can organize your list of resources in different ways, just by shuffling the deck.

For example, you might want to start by organizing your cards by resource: magazine articles, encyclopedias, books, newspapers, etc. Then, when you're in the magazine room of the library, you will have a quick and easy way to make sure you read all your magazine articles at the same time. Ditto for your trip to the newspaper reading room, the reference shelf and so on.

But at some point, you might want to have your list of resources organized in alphabetical order or separated into piles of resources you've checked and those you haven't. No problem: Just shuffle your cards again.

Even with the help of a computer, it would be time-consuming to do all of this on paper. The note card system is neater and more efficient, and that's the key to getting your work done as quickly and painlessly as possible!

I guarantee you'll win this card game

You're sitting in the library now, surrounded by a veritable bonanza of source materials for your paper. You've completed your bibliography cards. It's time to take notes. Here's how:

Write one thought, idea, quote or fact—and only one—on each card. There are no exceptions. If you encounter a very long quote or string of data, you can write on both the front and back of the card, if necessary. But *never* carry over a note to a second card. If you have an uncontrollable urge to do that, the quote is too long. If you feel that the author is making an incredibly good point, paraphrase it.

Write in your own words. Don't copy material word for word—you may inadvertently wind up plagiarizing when you write. Summarize key points or restate the material in your own words.

Put quotation marks around any material copied verbatim. Sometimes an author makes a point so perfectly, so poetically, you *do* want to capture it exactly as is. It's fine to do this on a limited basis. But when you do so, you must copy such statements *exactly*—every sentence, every word, every comma should be precisely as written in the original. And make sure you put quotation marks around this material. Don't rely on your memory to recall, later, which copy was paraphrased and which you copied verbatim.

Put the number of the corresponding bibliography card in the upper-left corner. This is the exact same number you put in the upper-left-hand corner of the bibliography card.

Include the page numbers (where you found the information) on the card. You can add this information under the resource number.

Write down the topic letter that corresponds to your preliminary outline. For example, the second section, "B," of your preliminary outline is about the French withdrawal from Vietnam. You found an interesting quote from a United States official that refers to this withdrawal. Write down the topic letter "B" in the upper right-hand corner of your note card. (You might come across interesting quotes or statistics that could add flavor and authority to your term paper, but you're not quite sure where they will fit in. Mark the card with an asterisk [*] or other symbol instead. Later, when you have a more detailed outline, you may discover where it fits.)

Give it a headline. Next to the topic letter, add a brief description of the information on the card. For example, your note card about the French withdrawal may read, "French Withdrawal: U.S. Comments."

As you fill out your note cards, be sure to transfer all information accurately. Always double-check names, dates and other statistics. The beauty of using the note-card system is that, once you've captured the information you need, you should never have to return to any of the sources a second time.

A note of caution here: While this system is terrific for helping you organize your time and your material, don't permit it to hamstring you if you find other interesting material.

As with the other exercises in note-taking, the index card system requires you not to be a *copyist*—you could have used the copy machine for that—but a *processor of information.*

Constantly ask yourself questions while looking at the source material:

Is the author saying this in such a way that I want to quote her directly, or should I paraphrase the material?

If you decide to paraphrase, you obviously don't have to write down the author's exact verbiage, and, therefore, can resort to some of the note-taking tips discussed in other chapters. The answer to this question will have a big impact on how much time it takes to fill in each index card.

Does this material support or contradict the arguments or facts of another author?

Who do I believe? If there *is* contradictory evidence, should I note it? Can I refute it? If it supports the material I already have, is it interesting or redundant?

Where does this material fit into my outline?

Often, source material won't be as sharply delineated as your plan for the term paper, which is why it is important to place *one and only one* thought on each card. Even though an author might place more than one thought into a paragraph, or even a sentence, you will be able to stick to your organizational guns if you keep your cards close to the outline vest.

You'll be superorganized

Before I came up with any term-paper research system in high school, my student life was, quite literally, a mess. I had pages and pages of notes for term papers, but sometimes I was unsure where quotes came from and whether or not they were direct quotes or paraphrases.

My photocopy system wasn't much of an improvement. Often, I would forget one piece of the bibliographic information I needed, necessitating yet another last-minute trip to the library. And organizing the voluminous notes when it came time to put my thoughts in order was worse than the researching and writing itself.

The card system will save you all of that grief. Writing one thought, idea, quote, etc., per card will eliminate the problems caused when disparate pieces of information appear on the same piece of paper. And writing the number of the source down before doing anything else will help you avoid any problems relating to proper attribution.

When you're ready to do your final outline, all you'll need to do is organize and reorder your cards until you have the most effective flow.

This simple note-card system is, in fact, one that many professional writers—including this one—swear by long after they leave the world of term papers and class reports behind.

Index